Journey to Wholeness:

The Path to God and Your True Self

To kevin,

with thanks for your

friendship, support +

all the fun we had

on our runs.

Harry Parker

&

Parson's Porch Books

www.parsonsporchbooks.com

Journey to Wholeness: The Path to God and Your True Self
ISBN: Softcover 978-1-949888-83-6
Copyright © 2019 by Harry Parker

Journey to Wholeness

Contents

Section Three
Side-trips on the Journey: Questions that Puzzle Us

Dedication

To my wife, Linda,

a gift from God who has made my life whole.

Preface

Nine years ago a thirty-second phone call changed my life. I was hosting the annual Christmas luncheon for our staff when I slipped out to get the results from a recent blood test. The voice on the other end of the line announced, "Your PSA is 3.5." The blood drained from my head as a bowling ball dropped into my stomach. Usually any number below 4.0 is considered normal. But I had undergone a prostatectomy six weeks earlier. My PSA should have been zero. No one had anticipated this. Everybody, and I mean everybody, had told me I would be fine. After all, the cancer had been caught early and my numbers were relatively low. But a retest a few days later confirmed our fears. I had metastatic prostate cancer for which there is no cure. My wife, my family and I were devastated.

As I sought to absorb this disquieting news, I was troubled by how fearful and anxious I felt. When I reached into my spiritual satchel for consolation, all I found were pennies, lint and a bus token. As a pastor, I thought I would be able to face such a trial with peace and confidence in God. In their absence I realized that my spirituality was a mile wide and an inch deep. Although I had observed daily devotions for decades, my prayer life, scripture study and overall discipleship were anemic at best.

This disease set me out on a pilgrimage to deepen my spiritual life. I began a quest to sift through a small mountain of books from the second to the twenty-first century. I drank deeply from the wells of wisdom dug by spiritual giants of the past, both ancient and modern. I have not "wasted my cancer" as pastor/theologian John Piper put it. As a result, I am in a different and better place. I have grown in my relationship with Christ, my understanding of the Gospel and my practice of spiritual disciplines. I have a deeper grasp of the Gospel and what it means to be a follower of Jesus. I identify with Augustine who confessed, "Late have I loved you, O Lord, late have I loved you." It is not an exaggeration to say that this illness has proved to be the worst thing that has ever happened to me as well as the source of some of the greatest blessings of my life. The passion in the autumn of my life is to share these life-changing discoveries with others that they might enter into wholeness of life as a Christ-follower. The pages that follow offer the gleanings of my discoveries as I have walked this rocky road.

My journey is best summarized in the words of the Psalmist.

> *"It was good for me that I was afflicted, that I might learn thy ways."*
> (Psalm 119:71)

Introduction

"Our hearts are unquiet, until they find rest in you, O God"
~St. Augustine

We are born with an innate desire for God. We all long to make connection with the Divine. This is true even of those who claim to be atheists. The author Julian Barnes spoke for many when he said, "I don't believe in God, but I miss him."

For some, this longing is profound, like that of a thirsty traveler in a parched desert. "As the deer longs for flowing streams, so my soul longs for you, O God" is the way the Psalmist put it. (Psalm 42:1)

For others this desire is more subtle. Theirs is the quiet sense that something is not quite right, that something is amiss.

This book offers guidance for those with "unquiet hearts" to find the wholeness of life that God intends for his children. The path that leads us to this destination begins with conversion to Christianity. The first unit, entitled "The Journey Begins – Becoming a Christian," is composed of five chapters that explain this process. The pilgrimage continues into the second section called "Roadmap for the Journey – The Spiritual Disciplines." By engaging in these practices we open ourselves to the Holy Spirit who not only transforms us into the likeness of Jesus, but also into our true and best selves. This is the subject of chapters six through fifteen. The final section, "Side-trips on the Journey – Questions that Puzzle Us" looks at questions commonly raised by those on the pilgrimage. These can be found in chapters sixteen through twenty-two.

Among those with "unquiet hearts" are professing Christians. We might believe in God but have not experienced the fullness of life that Christ offers. Many who sit in the pews every Sunday fit this description. We are practicing what has been coined as "nominal Christianity." This is the notion that being a Christian is largely a matter of confessing key doctrines and saying a simple prayer so that we will go to heaven when we die. But being a Christian is not merely a matter of believing certain things. It involves the decision to enter into a vital relationship with Jesus and to choose to live as his follower. This path is not always easy, but it is the best way to live. It alone can lead to wholeness of life.

Pope Gregory the Great (540 – 604) was one of the early Church Fathers whose influence charted the course of Christianity for centuries. Gregory was one of the most prolific writers of the Middle Ages. And yet, he never sought to be original or creative. His greatest pride was that he never said anything that had not been uttered first by the great teachers of earlier centuries.[1] Gregory's genius was to simplify, summarize and apply their ideas to practical life.

In the spirit of Gregory, I cannot claim much originality. The ideas that are shared in this book are the fruit of study and reflection over the past few years, drawing from the spiritual wisdom of the giants of our faith. Many might seem to be novel, but generally they do not represent new thoughts. Rather they reflect the recovery of forgotten and neglected truths.

---

[1] Gonzalez, Justo L. *The Story of Christianity: Vol I. The Early Church to the Dawn of the Reformation* (San Francisco: Harper & Row: 1984 p. 247.

Section One

The Journey Begins –
Becoming a Christian

Chapter One
Experiencing God's Love

My dad was a Baptist preacher. Throughout my childhood we went to church on both Sunday mornings and evenings. The evening services were informal and often included a time of testimony. The most common and popular testimonies were those where the speaker confessed the sordid tale of being a miserable alcoholic, wife-beater or thief. The storyteller recounted hitting bottom before attending a revival meeting where the gospel message was presented. It was as if a bolt of lightning struck. In the blink of an eye all taste for the bottle vanished, love was rekindled, and promises of restoration were sworn. It was dramatic and entertaining.

But as a young person who had already been baptized, I felt left out. I was a generally good kid, as I recall, who had professed his faith and been baptized at ten. I had never awoken in a gutter or spent the night in the county jail. But neither had I felt the electrical charge of the Holy Spirit coursing through my body. "What was wrong with me?" I wondered.

Although I do not question the sincerity of the testimonies, I am troubled by the implicit message. As a child I was convinced that a dramatic, powerful, instantaneous conversion was the norm. That had not been my experience and I therefore worried about my salvation. Not until later did I discover that conversion can take many forms.

For most people conversion is neither sudden nor dramatic. It is a gradual and gentle process. Methodist professor George Hunter's research reveals that the majority of converts take an average of two and one-half years to make a commitment to Christ. Loving Jesus and giving your life to him is seldom a rush job. This is true for most loving relationships. Although some people have experienced "love at first sight," this is the exception rather than the rule. The church has mistakenly lifted up Paul's Damascus Road conversion as normative.

The first five chapters of this text outline the Gospel story and a process for becoming a Christian. It assumes that the journey of faith takes time, effort and reflection. But this sojourn need not be burdensome. Though there are some challenging stretches, the path is generally pleasant and affirming as we discover our identity as God's child and the depths of his love for us.

Becoming a Christian involves more than saying a prayer, signing your name at the bottom of an evangelistic tract, or "Liking" Jesus on Facebook. A Christian is someone who has entered into a vital relationship with Jesus, knowing him as friend, Savior and Lord. But how does that happen? The process begins when we start to grasp how deeply we are loved by God.

Even those with only a nodding acquaintance of Christianity know that for Christians "God is love." (I John 4:8). It is one thing to say this, it is quite another to experience it. God's love is something we might believe in our minds, but not know in our hearts. Deep down we sense that God could not be bothered with the likes of us.

Church historian Richard Lovelace wrote,

Only a fraction of the present body of professing Christians are solidly appropriating the justifying work of Christ in their lives. Many...have a theoretical commitment to the doctrine, but in their day-to-day existence they rely on their sanctification for justification...Christians who are no longer sure that

God loves and accepts them in Jesus, apart from their present spiritual achievements, are subconsciously radically insecure persons.[2]

How can we come to know that we are loved by God; that we are God's beloved children? It takes some effort. This chapter offers three exercises that will help us know God's love in a personal way. These suggestions have been gleaned from the wisdom of spiritual guides over the ages. An experience of grace will probably not happen all at once. It is a gradual process. But little by little we will come to know God's love for us.

Many evangelistic techniques do not begin here. Their preferred method is to start by focusing on our sinfulness. But in scripture God's love and grace always precede any confrontation of sin. For example, in the book of Exodus we read that God delivered the Israelites from slavery in Egypt *before* he gave them the Law. He did not announce, "If you are very, very good and offer me lots of sacrifices, I will set you free." No, he set them free first and then gave instructions on how to live. We therefore begin our spiritual journey by getting in touch with the love of God.

Step One
Pray for an Experience of God's Love

The first and most important step is simply to ask God to reveal his love. God does not force himself on anyone and will not enter where he is not wanted. Our task is to seek, ask and open our lives.

The good news is that this is the kind of request God loves to grant! Paul tells us that "...God has poured out his love into our hearts by the Holy Spirit." (Romans 5:5) One of the primary works of the Holy Spirit is to fill us with the love of God. The process, as Augustine

[2] Lovelace, Richard F. *Dynamics of Spiritual Life: An Evangelical Theology of Renewal* (Downers Grove, Illinois: InterVarsisty, 1979) pp. 101, 211-212.

envisioned it, is that as we kneel in prayer for an experience of God's love, the Holy Spirit stands behind us and pours it into our minds and hearts. We are simply to open ourselves to the experience.

Give God an opportunity to reveal his love. "Make space for grace" by withdrawing from the noise and clutter. Seek out quiet and stillness. Take a hike in the woods or walk along the beach. Sit in a garden or take a drive in the country. The Benedictines advise doing mindless work, such as gardening, painting or dishwashing. Pay attention to the gentle ways in which God whispers his love. We are to be alert to ideas that pop into our minds or impressions that are laid upon our hearts.

"Neither knowing God nor knowing self can progress very far unless it begins with a knowledge of how deeply we are loved by God. Until we dare to believe that nothing can separate us from God's love...we remain in the elementary grades of the transformation."

David Brenner

An illustration of how this works is shared by Jesuit Spiritual Director William Barry in the story of a forty-year-old priest. The Father came to participate in a thirty-day retreat, somewhat against his will. He had grudgingly agreed, but the prospect of praying four or five hours a day for a month seemed daunting. More significantly, the idea that God would speak intimately to him was foreign. About the fourth day, however, he was "surprised by joy" to use C.S. Lewis's phrase. He woke up and sensed God saying, "You are precious in my eyes." Over the next few days he see-sawed between believing and doubting what had happened. But on the eighth day the reality of the experience sank in. Here was an encounter with God that he had long hoped for but did not expect.[3]

---

[3] Barry, William A., S.J. *Letting God Come Close: An Approach to the Ignatian Spiritual Exercises* (Chicago: Loyola Press, 2001) pp. 45, 46.

He experienced God's love because he persisted in opening himself to it.

Step Two
"Marinate" in the Stories and Promises of Scripture

The second step is to "marinate" in the promises of scripture. This term comes from Fr. Gregory Boyle who for years has worked with gang members in Los Angeles. On one occasion he was talking with a young man named Rascal about the love of God and read him some passages of scripture. The gang banger responded, "I'm gonna take that advice and I'm gonna let it marinate," pointing at his heart, "right here."[4]

We all need to "marinate" or soak in the stories and promises in the Bible. The Bible is known as God's Word. God speaks a personal message to us in and through it, if we take the time to listen.

Many, however, are handicapped by a negative image of God. We envision him as an ogre, a grumpy parent or a vindictive judge. Some think of him as cold, indifferent and aloof. It is hard to feel love from a character like that!

Reading the Bible can change that picture. For example, I Corinthians 13 is known as "the love chapter." It is read at nearly every wedding. But it can be used it in another way to great profit. Someone observed that since "God is love" (I John 4:8), we can substitute the word "God" every time we encounter the word "love." Now the chapter reads, "God is patient, God is kind. God does not envy, He does not boast, He is not proud. God is not rude or self-seeking. He is not easily angered and keeps no record of wrongs.

---

[4] Boyle, Fr. Gregory, *Tattoos on the Heart: The Power of Boundless Compassion* (New York: Simon & Schuster, 2010) p. 22.

God always protects, always trusts, always hopes, always perseveres. God never fails." That is the God that I would like to know better!

But perhaps the best way to experience God's love in scripture is to "marinate" in the stories of Jesus. Contemplate the incarnation, that is, that God became a human being in Jesus. How much love must it have taken to leave heaven to be born in a stable and grow up in a poor carpenter's home? Contemplate Jesus' teachings, especially stories like the parable of the Prodigal Son. Contemplate Jesus' deeds, particularly his healings and the friendship he extended to outcasts. Finally, contemplate Jesus' cross, the supreme demonstration of his love. Jesus took upon himself the shame and punishment we deserve. It is as if he walked into an oncology ward and said, "Give all your cancer to me. Give me your nausea, your weakness, and your fear. I will take it and suffer and die in your place."

Contemplating the cross can have a profound effect. The story is told of a group of young men who were horsing around outside of a cathedral. One of them dared another to enter the church and offer a false confession to the priest. Taking him up, the young man entered the confessional and began sharing some outlandish sins. At the end, he said to the priest, "Father, I need you to know that everything I just told you was a lie. It was all a joke. My friends bet me that I wouldn't do it and I had to prove them wrong." The priest thought for a moment and replied, "You seem to be a young man who likes a challenge. Very well, I will give you one. I dare you to go to the front of the sanctuary, stand before the crucifix, look Jesus in the eye and say out loud, 'You died for me, and I don't give a damn.'" The young man left the confessional, walked up to the altar, and stood silently before the cross for a few moments. Then he turned around and reentered the confessional. "Father," he said, "I am ready to make my confession."

The second step to experience God's love is to marinate in the stories and promises of scripture.

Step Three
Pay Attention to Our Lives

The third step is to pay attention to our lives. God's love is more easily *seen* than *felt*. That is to say, we experience the love of God by his actions more than by mystical feelings. That is the way it is with love. For example, my parents were not demonstrative in their affection and seldom hugged or said, "I love you." And yet I know that they did. I know that because every day my dad packed my lunch. Mom and Dad attended all of my concerts, plays, and cross country meets. They provided me with a safe and secure home. Their love for me was seen, rather than felt. But it is in remembering and contemplating those acts of love that I feel their affection.

The same is true in the spiritual realm. God's love is better seen than felt. This is why we need to open our eyes to the many ways that God shows his love in everyday life. Paying attention to these gifts of love, along with gratitude for them, are the portals that open us up to a deeper relationship with God.

In an ancient monastic tale, a traveler begged the Teacher for a word of wisdom. The Teacher, who had taken a vow of silence, smiled and wrote a single word on a sheet of paper. The word was "Awareness." The traveler was a bit perplexed and said, "That is far too brief an answer. Can you not expand on it a bit?" The Teacher took the paper, turned it over and wrote, "Awareness, awareness, awareness." "But what does that mean?" demanded the traveler. The Teacher reached for the paper and wrote, clearly and firmly, "Awareness, awareness, awareness means…Awareness!"[5]

God is far more present and involved in our lives than we could ever imagine. Every day he sends gifts of love. In fact, the Bible says that *every* good and perfect gift comes from above. But he likes to operate incognito. His gifts tend to be small, everyday blessings that can be easily overlooked. Things like a morning conversation with our spouse, a hug from a child, the taste of a juicy peach, an "Atta boy" from the boss, a yellow daffodil in our garden, an orange sunset, etc. He lavishes his love on us. As former Fuller Seminary President Richard Mouw is fond of saying, "God is not stingy, but generous." He does not dispel his love with an eye dropper but pours it out in buckets.

There is a purpose for this gifting. St. Francis of Assisi taught that every good thing comes *from* God and is designed to lead us *to* God. To paraphrase something he said, "The beauty and wonder of nature are footprints that lead us to God." We can expand this to say that every gift from God is a footprint that leads us to God. God's good gifts are like the trail of Reese's Pieces that Elliot left for E.T. to lead him to his bedroom.

Although every day God lavishes his love, it might be missed in the moment. God's gifts of love are most easily seen in retrospect. It is in looking back and examining our lives that we begin to notice the many ways that God has showered his love in tangible, concrete ways both great and small.

We can come to recognize this by simply retracing our steps throughout the day. Notice those times when something good

---

[5] Chittister, Joan, *Wisdom Distilled from the Daily: Living the Rule of St. Benedict Today* (San Francisco: Harper & Row, 1990), p. 68.

happened. Remember, these are often small things. See them as a gift of love from our Father in heaven. Look upon them as evidence and reminders of God's goodness and care. The Prayer of Examen, which we will look at in depth in a later chapter, is a tool that many have found to be of immeasurable help in recognizing God's daily gifts of love.

On a larger scale, we walk through the years of our lives, recalling significant events. We look for things such as people who touched us and changed our lives, accomplishments of which we are proud, times when we were rescued from danger or death, disappointments that turned out to be great blessings, doors that unexpectedly opened or closed, surprises and "flukes" that redirected our lives. Those are examples of God working in our lives.

We can accomplish something similar by walking the Labyrinth. Nearly every community has one, usually at a Roman Catholic or other liturgical church. A Labyrinth looks like a circular maze, but one in which we can never get lost. Following the twisting and turning path will eventually lead us to the center and then out again. The Labyrinth is a tool for contemplation. It offers a way of literally walking through our lives. At each twist, we pause and recall a turning point in our lives. In our early lives it might have been a teacher, a friend or a move to a new city. We continue on throughout all of our years. We seek God's hand in these moments.

Our Jewish brothers and sisters have a wonderful practice that we can adapt. At the Passover meal they sing a song that is called "Dayenu." The word means "It would have been enough." The lines include a litany of all the things God did to deliver them. They sing, "It would have been enough that we escaped from Egypt, but he gave us the gold and silver of our captors. It would have been enough to allow us to pass through the Red Sea, but he also provided bread, water and meat in the wilderness..." Walk through your life and compose your own Dayenu. "It would have been enough that God gave me life, but he also gave me a healthy body. It would have been enough that I was accepted into college, but he also provided me with a scholarship..."

As you look back over your life you might find yourself joining with Jacob who dreamed of a stairway leading to heaven. When he awoke, he said, "Surely the Lord was in this place, and I knew it not.

Exercises

Step One: Ask to Experience God's Love

- Pray that the Holy Spirit would fill you with God's love

- Open yourself to this experience by stilling your mind and finding a place of quiet and solitude

- Pay attention to ideas that come into your head, impressions that enter your heart, or anything else that whispers to you of God's love

Step Two: "Marinate" in Scripture

God speaks a personal word to you in and through the pages of the Bible. He wants to address you personally in countless passages. The verses that are listed below offer good starting points to experience God's love. Take time to slowly read and reread each day's verses. To which words or phrases are you drawn? Which ones gently stand out or "shimmer" for you? Meditate on that word or phrase. What is God saying to you? If helpful, use the questions below as a guide or starter.[6] (These exercises are based on the "Principle and Foundation" step of the Spiritual Exercises of Ignatius of Loyola.)

Day One

How great is the love the Father has lavished on us, that we should be called Children of God! And that is what we are! (I John 3:1)

- In what way or ways is God's love "great"?

- How has God lavished his love on you?

- What does it mean that you are a "Child of God"?

Day Two

I pray that you, being rooted and established in love, may have power, together with all the saints, to grasp how wide and long and high and deep is the love of Christ, and to know this love that surpasses knowledge, that you might be filled to the measure of the fullness of God. (Ephesians 3:17-19)

- What does it mean when it says God's love is wide? Long? High? Deep?

- What does it mean to be "rooted and established in love"?

- What do you think is "love that surpasses knowledge"?

Day Three

You see, at just the right time, when we were still powerless, Christ died for the ungodly. God demonstrates his own love for

---

[6] Adapted from: Warner, Larry. *Journey with Jesus: Discovering the Spiritual Exercises of Saint Ignatius.* (Downers Grove, Illinois: InterVarsity Press, 2010), pp. 63-75.

us in this: While we were still sinners, Christ died for us.
(Romans 5:6, 8)

• In what ways are you "powerless"?

• What are some of the ways God reveals his love for you?

• What does this text say is the primary way he demonstrates his love for you?

• What does this passage tell you about the unconditional nature of God's love for you?

Day Four

The Lord is my shepherd, I shall not want. He makes me lie down in green pastures, he leads me beside quiet waters, he restores my soul. He leads me in paths of righteousness for his name's sake. Yea, though I walk through the valley of the shadow of death, I will fear no evil, for you are with me; your rod and your staff, they comfort me. You prepare a table before me in the presence of my enemies. You anoint my head with oil, my cup overflows. Surely goodness and mercy will follow me all the days of my life, and I will dwell in the house of the Lord forever. (Psalm 23)

• What difference does it make to you to know that God is your shepherd?

• Imagine lying in green pastures beside quiet waters. What feelings does that evoke?

• What shadows are falling across your path?

• How does God's rod and staff comfort you?

• Imagine God anointing your head with oil. What does that do for you?

Day Five

But now, this is what the Lord says — he who created you, O Jacob, he who formed you, O Israel: "Fear not, for I have redeemed you; I have summoned you by name; you are mine; When you pass through the waters, I will be with you; and when you pass through the rivers, they will not sweep over you. When you walk through the rivers, they will not sweep over you. When you walk through the fire, you will not be burned; the flames will not set you ablaze. For I am the Lord, your God, the Holy One of Israel, your Savior." (Isaiah 43:1-3)

• What difference does it make to you to know that you were created by God?

• What difference does it make to know that God has redeemed you and declared, "You are mine"?

• What deep waters and fiery trials are you facing?

• How would your life be different if you knew these promises were true?

Day Six

If God is for us, who can be against us? He who did not spare his own Son, but gave him up for us all — how will he not also, along with him, graciously give us all things? Who can separate us from the love of Christ? Shall trouble or hardship or persecution or famine or nakedness or sword? No, in all these things we are more than conquerors through him who loves us. For I am convinced that neither death nor life, neither angels nor demons, neither the present nor the future, nor any powers, neither height nor depth, nor anything else in all creation will be able to separate us from the love of God that is in Christ Jesus our Lord. (Romans 8:31-32, 35-39)

• Who or what is against you? How does the power of that threat measure up to the power of God?

• What does it mean to you that God did not spare his Son, but freely gave him for you? How hard would that be? What does that say to you?

• What are some things that are trying to separate you from God's love?

• What difference would it make if you knew in your heart of hearts that there was nothing that could keep you from God's love?

Step Three: Pay Attention to Your Life

• Every day, at the end of each day, walk through your waking hours, looking for examples of God's daily gifts of love

• Take a weekend and spend time retracing the years of your life, looking for evidence of God's guiding hand

• Walk the Labyrinth

• Create your own "Dayenu" prayer

For further reading

William A. Barry, "Letting God Come Close"

Richard Peace, "Spiritual Autobiography"

Larry Warner, "Journey with Jesus" (Part 2 Preparatory Exercises)

Phillip Yancey, "What's So Amazing About Grace?"

Discussion Guide

1. Tell the students that you are going to help them get in touch with the imaginative/creative side of their brains. Invite them to close their eyes and imagine that they are sitting in a theatre, staring up at a blank screen. As the lights are going down, you will speak a word and ask them to watch what happens on the screen of their imagination. The word is "Fall." Allow them one or two minutes of contemplation. Ask them to share what they saw. (Typically answers include an autumn day, falling off a cliff or The Fall in Genesis.)

2. Do the same exercise a second time, but this time use the word "God." Ask people to share what they saw and what they felt. (Typically there will be a wide range of answers from a loving shepherd to wrathful judge.) Ask people where they think this image came from.

3. Point out that the first step in becoming a follower of Jesus is to discover how deeply they are loved by God. This is difficult for many people, since their image of God is anything but loving. Why do so many people know that "God is love" in a theoretical but not an experiential way?

4. Indicate to the group that an experience of God's love generally requires some effort on their part. One exercise is to simply ask for it. Remind them of Augustine's image of the Holy Spirit pouring God's love into us as we pray for it. Also share with them the story of the priest on a spiritual retreat. Ask the group to break up and go to a

quiet corner, praying for an experience of God's love and waiting for it. After a few minutes, gather them back to share. Generally little, if anything, will have happened. This prayer, however, is something that is meant to be practiced on a daily basis. Challenge them to try it for a month and see what happens.

5. Scripture is a tool that reveals God's love. Invite the group to return to the theatre and close their eyes as you slowly read I Corinthians 13, substituting "God" for every time you come across the word "love." Invite them to share their experiences.

6. God's love is more easily seen than felt. He sends gifts of love to us every day. But these are often small gifts that are easily overlooked. Invite the group to retire to a quiet corner and walk through their previous twenty-four hours, taking note of the good things God gave them in the day before. Regroup and share. Typically people are amazed at how much good happened to them. Remind them that these are evidences of God's goodness and love.

7. Return to the theatre one last time. This time the word they are to focus on is "Jesus." How did what they saw compare with what they observed when the word was "God?" Point out that Jesus is none other than the full and perfect revelation of God. The more people know Jesus, the more they will experience God and his love.

Chapter Two
Recognizing Our Sin

It was a sinister but effective ploy, conjured up by a semi-evil genius. I detected it soon after I began working at Madigan's Department Store while in seminary. A ten-foot-wide floor-to-ceiling mirror had been installed directly across from the down escalator. As customers slowly descended, they could not avoid seeing their reflection. I could almost read their minds. "Is that what I look like? I had no I idea! I dress like a flood victim. I need to buy some new clothes." Salespeople circled like friendly sharks waiting to make the kill.

> *"A mirror shows us the shape of our nose and the curve of our chin, things we otherwise know only through the reports of others. The Psalms show us the shape of our souls and the curve of our sin, realities deep within us, hidden and obscured for which we need focus and names."*
>
> *Eugene Peterson*

Most of us do not know what we really look like, on the outside or in. It is difficult to know our true selves. My dad had a line from Scottish poet Robert Burns framed for his desk. "O would some power the gift gives us, to see ourselves as others see us." It is not until we see our reflection that we recognize our true selves. Our physical appearance is revealed by a mirror. Our spiritual condition becomes apparent only as we take a close look at ourselves in light of the biblical revelation of our human condition. How to do that is the subject of this chapter.

The second step in becoming a Christian is recognizing and admitting our sinfulness. Scripture teaches that "all have sinned and fallen short of the glory of God." (Romans 3:23) But we resist acknowledging this. If we ask a random passerby, "What kind of person are you?" he would no doubt reply, "I think I am a pretty good person." This is because sin blinds us to our own sinfulness. The Psalmist observed, "In their own eyes they flatter themselves too much to detect or hate their sin " (Psalm 36:2)

It is not pleasant to be confronted by our sins. And yet an awareness of our sinfulness is ultimately a gift because it alone can lead to a deeper experience of God's love and grace. It is only when we know the depths of our fallenness that we can appreciate what God has done for us. Only the prodigal son, not his elder brother, came to know the depths of his father's love.

But we must proceed with caution. There is an inherent risk in examining our sinfulness and failure. It can lead to discouragement, hopelessness and a sense of worthless. We are vulnerable to this if we have not first grasped how deeply we are loved by God.

It is important to note that there is a difference between conviction of sin, sometimes called "godly sorrow," and a sense of condemnation or shame. Conviction is feeling bad or guilty about something we have *done*. Condemnation or shame is feeling bad about who we *are*. If we feel condemned, we can be assured that it is not of God. Sinking into these feelings is a sign that we need to back off and spend time bathing in God's love. Ignatius of Loyola would not permit his sensitive friend, Peter Favre, to examine his sinfulness for four years! Such was his need to first be grounded in God's love.

What is Sin?

If we are going to examine our lives for sinfulness, we need to know what we are looking for. We usually think of sin as breaking the rules, violating laws or disobeying commandments. We associate it with doing bad things like lying, stealing, cursing or sleeping around. While these are sinful behaviors, they are more symptoms than the disease itself. Sin is not so much something we do as it is a state that we are in. The state of sin is the condition of being estranged and alienated from God. In Romans, Paul indicated that the essence of sin is loving the created things of the world more than the creator himself. This is sometimes referred to as having "disordered affections."

An image that is helpful is "center of gravity." We need to ask ourselves where the center of gravity is in our lives. Is it with ourselves, that is, our wants and desires? Or is it with someone or something outside of ourselves that has captured our hearts? It could be something like our jobs, our degrees, or our power. Having other people or things as our center of gravity is the definition of idolatry. That issue will be dealt with at greater length in a later chapter. Wholeness is only discovered when God is our center of gravity.

The story of Adam and Eve is instructive. This first pair had everything their hearts could desire. God had provided them with a literal paradise. He showered them with good things of the Garden, including the gift of himself. Life was bliss. But Adam and Eve were not content. They wanted more. They desired to be the gods of their own lives. They wanted to run things, to call the shots and to do whatever they wished. In essence, they wanted to be God. And so they rejected the Lord and placed themselves on the thrones of their lives.

This is not a story about two people who lived a long time ago in a land far away. This is our story. We are Adam and Eve. Their sin is our sin. The story teaches us that the essence of sin is turning our backs on God. This is the sin from which all other sins derive. At its heart, sin is self-centeredness. Maybe we haven't completely rejected God, but we have put him on the periphery of our lives. He has been relegated to the sidelines. We are the quarterback, while God sits on the bench waiting to be put in the game when things get desperate.

When we reject or sideline God, we are drawn to acts of sin like a magnet. Something within the human heart gravitates to the dark side. The state of sin manifests itself in all kinds of wrong behaviors. For Adam and Eve it was eating the forbidden fruit. For us it can include overtly evil deeds such as lying, cheating, and stealing. But it also reveals itself in less obvious and more "acceptable" sins such as gossiping, selfishness, manipulation, insensitivity, stubbornness, judgmentalism, etc. The Seven Deadly Sins are Pride, Anger, Greed, Lust, Gluttony, Sloth, and Envy. Our hearts could be filled with all seven, and no one would be the wiser.

Many of us have attempted to expunge sinful acts from our lives and found it a futile exercise. We might succeed for a while, but soon we find ourselves slipping back into old habits. This is because when we give into sin it gains strength over us until we are unable to resist. The more we succumb, the greater its grasp, just as the more a heroin addict shoots up, the firmer the drug's clutches. Sin has no power beyond what we give to it. But once it has its hold on us, we become increasingly powerless. Our puny efforts are no match against its grip. Try as we might, we continue to fall back into our old habits.

The popular preacher Tony Evans tells a story that illustrates our dilemma. He had purchased a new home when he discovered a crack in the wall. He called a handyman who patched and painted the wall. It looked perfect. But two weeks later, the crack returned. Evans called the worker to redo the work, which he did. Two weeks later, the crack again reappeared. For a third time the handyman was called. This time he stared at the wall and said, "There is nothing I can do. The problem is not the wall, it is your foundation. You will never be able to fix the cracks until you repair your foundation."

Our individual sins are like the cracks that indicate our foundation is faulty. They are symptoms of a more serious illness. The real issue is that we have built our lives around ourselves rather than on the Rock.

Augustine considered the greatest sin of his life to be when he stole some pears from his neighbor's tree. On the surface, it was a youthful petty crime. But Augustine knew better. The theft symbolized how sinful he was. He stole, not because he was hungry, but because he knew it was wrong. Violating the law pleased him. No one was going to tell him what to do! He derived even greater pleasure from knowing that his deed hurt and angered the neighbor. He delighted in his transgression. It was not until years later that Augustine came to recognize the depths of sinfulness that was represented by stealing that forbidden fruit. In a similar vein, our seemingly insignificant acts of sin speak volumes of our rebellion against our Maker. We would benefit by following Augustine's example to examine the deeper significance of our sins.

What is sin? It is living a life turned away from God. It is not so much a violation of a law as a broken relationship.

How to Recognize Our Sin

How can we come to recognize sin in our lives? It is not easy! As mentioned earlier, it is a spiritual reality that sin blinds us to our own sinfulness. This is especially true of "good people." For one thing, we tend not to commit any of the more obvious sins like murder, adultery, or stealing. Therefore, from the outside we appear to be straight arrows. In addition, we often rationalize or relabel our sin as a virtue. Greed becomes competitiveness, ruthlessness becomes good business practice, willfulness becomes strong leadership, etc. Finally, in our minds our good deeds outshine and outweigh any shortcomings. And so we walk around confidently singing the children's song, "There ain't no flies on me, there ain't no flies on me. There might be flies on some of you guys, but there ain't no flies on me."

Only God can reveal our sins to us. Therefore, one of the first works of the Holy Spirit is to convict us of our failures. We can cooperate with the Holy Spirit by engaging in the following exercises. These mirror the three exercises in Chapter One on "Experiencing God's Love". These include

Step One: Praying that Our Eyes be Opened

Because sin blinds us to our own sinfulness, we need the revealing work of the Holy Spirit to open our eyes, so we can recognize our transgressions. We receive that help when we ask for it and then open ourselves to receive it.

Step Two: Meditate on Scripture

Scripture can function like a mirror, revealing flaws that otherwise are invisible to us. The Bible is a tool that identifies sinful behavior and helps us to recognize where we are in error. This is the point that Eugene Peterson made in the quote above.

Step Three: Examine Our Lives

It is easy for sins to slip by us. Our transgressions are often best seen in the rear-view mirror. It is in looking back over our day and our past that we can see where we have gone wrong.

These exercises are included at the end of this chapter.

As we go through these exercises we discover that we are far more sinful than we ever imagined. Like Paul, we might conclude that "I am the worst of sinners." I recall when this happened to me. Every morning I take my dog for a two-mile walk. I use this time for prayer and reflection. For several days I had been practicing the third step of examining my life when the buried memory of some of my earlier transgressions came to the surface. I was deeply troubled by things I had done. For the first time I realized how selfish and self-centered I had been and how I had hurt innocent people. Paul might have been the chief of sinners, but in that moment I felt that I came in a close second.

Why Bother?

All this self-examination can be depressing. So why put so much time and effort into something that will only make us feel bad? At least three reasons stand out.

"Awareness of one's sinfulness is important for spiritual growth. That is why Anthony de Mello wrote, 'Be grateful for your sins. They are carriers of grace.'"

James Martin

1. Self-examination stops the hurt

Sin is destructive. The reason we are told not to do certain things is because of the harm they cause to ourselves and others. Sin has consequences. When we sow the wind, we reap the whirlwind. We might be able to get away with it for a season, but eventually our sins will find us out. It is like driving the wrong way on the expressway. A person might be able travel for a long distance with no incidents, but sooner or later there is bound to be a terrible wreck.

That is why God provides us with guilt. In our day and age guilt is considered a bad thing. We try to escape or ignore it. But a sense of guilt is a gift. It is a sign that something is wrong. Guilt tells us that we are treading on dangerous ground. Guilt functions like the taste of poison. The bitterness tells us to spit it out. Pay attention to guilty feelings. They are our friends!

2. Self-examination helps us understand that we are "Loved Sinners"

The exercises of chapters one and two are designed to bring us to an understanding of our fundamental identity. That identity is as Loved Sinners. We need to understand both parts. It is not enough for us to know that we are loved by God. This could lead to narcissism or complacency. It is not enough to know that we are sinners. That would lead to despair. As Presbyterian minister Tim Keller is fond of saying, "The Gospel tells that we are far more sinful than we ever imagined, but also far more loved than we ever dreamed possible."

Such an understanding renders us humble. Humility saves us from the deadliest of all sins, which is pride. Jay Leno once said, "I think the key to life is low self-esteem – believing you're not the smartest or most handsome person in the room. All the people who have high self-esteem are criminals and actors."

The story is told of a man who came to his first A.A. meeting. He was impeccably dressed and introduced himself as a graduate of a prestigious university and an officer in a Fortune 500 company. One of those present leaned over to his neighbor and whispered, "I used to be like that myself, until I achieved low self-esteem."

We all need to achieve appropriate low self-esteem, i.e., the humility that comes from knowing that we are Loved Sinners.

3. Self-examination makes us right with God

The most important reason for self-examination is that a consciousness of our sinfulness can usher us into a right relationship with God. Until we know how sinful we are we have no need for a Savior. We are like the Prodigal Son while he still had money in his pockets. It was only when he lost everything that he realized what he had done and started out on the road home. An awareness of our sinfulness puts us on the road back to God.

Before the prodigal even reached home, his father spotted him. He ran out to him, embraced him, kissed him, put a robe on his shoulders, shoes on his feet, a ring on his finger and killed the fatted calf. This is the picture of how God receives us. He does not do so reluctantly or grudgingly, but enthusiastically. As mentioned earlier, only a prodigal knows the depths of a father's love, something the elder brother could never grasp. This is why Anthony de Mello said, "Be grateful for your sins. They are carriers of grace."

Jonathan Edwards wrote, "There is a difference between believing that God is holy and gracious, and having a new sense on the heart of the loveliness and beauty of that holiness and grace. The difference between believing that God is gracious and tasting that God is gracious is as different as having a rational belief that honey is sweet and having the actual sense of its sweetness."

We taste that sweetness only after we have come face to face with our sinfulness. The following are exercises that offer guidance in that process.

Exercises

I. Pray that Your Eyes be Opened

Begin by asking God to open your eyes to your sins. Then take time to listen to the Holy Spirit speak to you. Because God tends to speak in a still small voice, you need to be quiet. Take a walk on the beach or in the forest. Sit in a garden or a quiet corner. Engage in some mindless work. Pay attention to ideas that come into your mind, impressions that come onto your heart, conversations, coincidences and things you read. If you know you are loved by God, this conviction of sin will lead to "godly sorrow" rather than condemnation. Remember, a sense of condemnation is not of God!

II. Meditate on Scripture[7]

The stories in the Bible are not just about people who lived a long time ago in a land far away. They are *our* stories. We share their sins and failures. We are the Israelites murmuring in the desert, David cavorting with Bathsheba, or Peter denying Jesus. Meditate on these stories, seeking to recognize your place in them.

Day One – Genesis 3:1-19

• What was their sin(s)? To what extent is that your sin?

• Why is taking a piece of fruit so serious? Why did it represent? What do your individual sins represent?

• What did they do when confronted by God? Do you ever feel that way?

• What were the consequences of their sin? Why so severe? What consequences have you suffered?

Day Two – Exodus 20:1-11

• How well have you obeyed these commandments? Fully? Half-heartedly? Not at all? Why?

• To what extent have you broken these in spirit, if not in letter?

• What has lured you away from God and obedience?

---

[7] Adapted from Warner, Larry. *Journey with Jesus: Discovering the Spiritual Exercises of Saint Ignatius* (Downers Grove, Illinois: InterVarsity, 2010)

Day Three – Exodus 20: 12-17

• How well have you obeyed these commandments? Fully? Half-heartedly? Not at all? Why?

• To what extent have you broken them in spirit, if not in letter?

• What has lured you away from God and obedience?

Day Four – James 1:13-15

• What is the progression that James describes?

• Where in your life have you seen sin take hold like this?

• Where are you struggling with temptation? What are the desires and disordered attachments with which you are wrestling?

Day Five – Mark 9:43-48

• What does this passage say about the seriousness of sin?

• Do you take the destructive nature of your sin this seriously? Why or why not?

• Are there sins in your life that need to be cut out?

• Ask God to help you discover the desires within that are giving birth to those sins and for freedom from them.

Day Six – Luke 18:9-14

• Both men are sinners. With whom do you identify?

• Let your sins of commission and omission as well as your sinful tendencies float through your mind.

• Spend time repeating the phrase, "God, have mercy on me, a sinner."

III. Examine Your Life

Walk through your previous day, paying attention for the times when you committed what are called "sins of commission." Were you short or hurtful to someone? Did you have evil thoughts? Did you take something that did not belong to you? Were you lazy, neglectful or self-centered? Did you look down on other people? Did you rationalize something you said or did? Pay attention also to "sins of omission." Were there things you could have done, but failed to do so? When did you not bother? Look back over the years of your life. When have you committed sins of omission or commission?

For further reading:

Larry Warner, "Journey with Jesus" (Part 3: The Spiritual Exercises, Week 1: Sin, Me and God's Love)

Discussion Guide

1. Play a word association game. After each word, have the class write down three words that pop into their minds. The words are:

- Play
- Star
- Sin

2. What is sin? If an alien came to earth and had no concept of the term, what would you say?

3. Read silently the section "What is Sin?" Discuss the concept of sin as a state that we are in, rather than something we do.

4. Review what Augustine considered his greatest sin. What made it so bad in his eyes? Was he right? Recall a similar petty crime or offense from your youth. What did your actions represent?

5. Prepare and distribute a copy of the Ten Commandments. Invite the group to find a quiet corner to silently read and reflect on ways they have disobeyed them, either in letter or spirit. When they regroup ask if anyone would share a discovery.

6. What are some of the consequences of sin? Who gets hurt? What gets damaged?

7. What is the difference between guilt and shame? How do you overcome shame?

8. Remind the class that the ultimate purpose of these exercises is not to feel bad, but to experience in a new way the grace of God. Only a prodigal knows the depths of his father's love.

Chapter Three
The Rescue Mission

On August 5, 2010 a massive explosion in Chile trapped thirty-three miners a half-mile deep in the earth. The blast cut off their only means of escape. It was one of the worst mining disasters in the country's history. No one above ground knew if there were any survivors. What they did know was that the clock was ticking. If the miners were still alive, they only had days before they exhausted their water and oxygen supplies. If the miners were to be saved, the rescuers would need to do three things. First, they had to locate them. Second, they had to find a way to deliver oxygen, food and water. Third, they would have to drill an escape shaft to extricate them. Amazingly, twelve days after the collapse, a drill broke through at the exact spot where the thirty-three had taken shelter. The borehole soon began supplying their essential needs. Sixty-nine days later a larger shaft was completed and a rescue capsule brought the first miner to the top. Eventually all thirty-three miners were saved! The rescue mission had been a success.

Two thousand years ago there was another kind rescue mission. It was God's rescue of the world that was in the clutches of evil and sin. Just as there were three phases to the Chilean mission, so there were three stages to God's strategy. The first took place on Good Friday when Jesus died on the cross. The second occurred three days later on Easter Sunday when God raised Jesus from the dead. The third was fifty days later on the Day of Pentecost when the Holy Spirit was poured out on all believers. Together these events collaborated to secure God's rescue mission of humanity.

Rescue from What?

Before we explore God's three-fold strategy, we need to understand why such a mission was necessary in the first place. The reasons were alluded to in the previous chapter. It boils down to sin and its consequences. Recall that the essence of sin is usurping God's rightful place in our lives, deciding to live on our own terms. It is basically self-centeredness and pride. Such egocentricity leads us to commit all kinds of individual, specific sins. It is the violation of the commandments that God gave for our benefit.

Choices have consequences. The prophet warns us that when we sow the wind, we reap the whirlwind. (Hosea 8:7) It might not happen right away, but sooner or later the bill comes due. The following are some of the major consequences for our sinfulness. They explain why we need deliverance and rescue.

Estrangement from God

Whereas once Adam and Eve enjoyed intimate friendship with God, everything changed when they violated their limited creatureliness, represented by eating the forbidden fruit. Now they were afraid and hid from God. He had become a threat to be avoided. Their sin destroyed the fellowship they had once enjoyed. When we sin, we become estranged from God. Instead of companionship, we are alienated and afraid of him. In our minds he has become an enemy, not a friend. We seek to escape God, not draw close.

Strife with One Another

Sin also wrecked Adam and Eve's relationship with one another. When confronted with their transgressions they began to accuse one another. "It's your fault!" "No, you are the one to blame!" Such estrangement snowballed into violence in the next generation. Their son, Cain, murdered his brother, Abel, because of jealousy and resentment. This is what happens when people live for themselves. We are at enmity with each other.

Sin's Unbreakable Hold

Sin cannot force itself on us. All it can do is tempt, but when we give into the temptation, sin gains a hold over us. Every time we sin, it gathers strength until it rules us. Before long it is a habit. Finally it becomes irresistible. C.S. Lewis compared committing sin to walking into a swamp. Every step takes us farther and deeper into the muck until we cannot extricate ourselves. We become stuck and powerless to resist.

Shame and Condemnation

When we sin, it is natural for us to experience guilt. This is not a bad thing. Guilt is an uncomfortable feeling that tells us something is wrong. But such healthy guilt can descend into feelings of shame and condemnation. This is the work of the enemy. Satan first tempts us to do wrong. Then he uses our sins against us. It is no accident that he is called "The Accuser" because that is what he does. He tells us that we are no better than the worst thing we have ever done. Our sins define us. They become our identity. If we lie, he tells us that we are nothing but liars. If we cheat, by definition we are cheaters. To fail means that we are failures. Whereas guilt tells us that we *did* something bad, shame tells us that we *are* bad. The Enemy capitalizes on these feelings and whispers, "God could never forgive or love someone like you." Satan wants us to feel worthless and unlovable.

Suffering

God prohibits certain behaviors because they are harmful to us or others. In Romans 1 we are told that God's wrath is kindled when we violate his will. But his judgment is not to be seen in lightning bolts from heaven or painful boils on our body. Instead he simply gives up on us. God is pained by what we do to ourselves and others, and yet allows us the freedom to have our destructive way. When we act contrary to God's purposes, he allows us to receive the natural consequences of our choices. So if we choose to smoke two packs of cigarettes a day for thirty years, he will let us. But we dare not be surprised if we develop asthma, emphysema or cancer. If we are determined to cheat on our marriage vows, he will not stop us. But we will pay the price in a broken home, financial ruin and the loss of the respect of family and friends. God does not punish us *for* our sins, rather we are punished *by* them.

Eternal Judgment

Jesus speaks frequently about the serious consequences of living life outside of, or in direct violation of, the will of God. He drives that seriousness home when he evokes the horror of the "Valley of Hinnom" (Greek "Gehenna" from which we get the English word "Hell") which was located south of the Temple. Gehenna was Jerusalem's garbage dump, perpetually burning and smoldering. Whether Jesus meant that as a literal place or whether he used it as a symbol is a question which Christians have debated for centuries. One thing is certain: Life apart from a relationship with God, the giver and sustainer of authentic life, is a deadly life in the here and now, and an eternal death in the future.

These, then, are the consequences of our sin. All of them are the result of our free choice to reject God and live life outside of his good purposes for us.

Phase One
Good Friday – Jesus' Death on the Cross

It is amazing that God does not abandon us to wallow in the mess we have made. He does not wash his hands of us and say, "They made their bed. Now let them lie in it." Instead he launches a rescue mission to deliver and save us.

The first phase of the rescue mission took place on Good Friday with Jesus' death on the cross. On the cross Jesus took upon himself all the sin, guilt, shame, embarrassment and punishment we deserve. He became "the Lamb of the God who takes away the sin of the world." He paid the price for our sin. As a result, we are forgiven and cleansed of all our unrighteousness.

We are more than just forgiven; however, we are justified. The difference between the two is subtle, but significant. To forgive means to pardon. The offender is still guilty but has been shown mercy. To be justified means that the sin has been completely wiped away.

> *"While we were yet sinners, Christ died for the ungodly"*
>
> *Romans 5:6*

My understanding of justification came as a result of one of the more painful episodes of my life. I had been invited to a dinner party and was seated next to an acquaintance who I did not know very well. In the course of the evening she asked me about my children. I enthusiastically recounted all their accomplishments. To be honest, I was bragging. I felt vaguely uncomfortable after our conversation, but on the way home I was horrified by what I had said. For I remembered that my new friend's son, who was the same age as my children, had died under tragic circumstances near his graduation from high school.

My words must have been like a knife in her heart. I called the next day and apologized profusely. She was gracious and forgiving. But I did not want forgiveness. What I wanted was for it never to have happened. And that is when I began to understand justification.

The preacher Fleming Rutledge observed that justification includes forgiveness, but it is also more than forgiveness. With forgiveness the stain and the sting remain, for both the perpetrator and the innocent victim. But with justification, in God's eyes the offense never occurred. God has divine amnesia and forgets our sin. It is as if it had never occurred. John the Baptist did not say of Jesus, "Behold the Lamb of God who *forgives* the sins of the world." He said, "Behold the Lamb of God who *takes away* the sins of the world." Interestingly enough, the Apostle Paul seldom characterizes Jesus' work as forgiveness. His preferred description is justification.

Justification robs Satan of one of his most lethal weapons. He really only has two. The first is temptation. The Enemy attempts to seduce us into transgression. Once we succumb, he brings out the big gun of accusation. The word Satan means "Accuser" for that is what he does. He accuses us of being no better than the worst thing we have ever done. Our sins define us. But on the cross Jesus strips Satan of this sword. The accusations and attacks fall flat. They are no longer true, for Jesus has justified us. We are no longer guilty, but innocent.

In Martin Luther's hymn, "A Mighty Fortress is our God" there is a line about how "one little word" shall fell Satan. What is that little word? Luther himself gave the answer. It is "Liar." When the devil comes calling with his false promises and accusations, we can rebuke him by calling him "Liar." And since he hates to be mocked, we can rub it in by singing, "Liar, liar, pants on fire!"

It is difficult to understand how the cross works. How is it possible that all the sins of the world were transferred to Jesus? This is a great mystery that is beyond our comprehension. I was encouraged when I took a class in Hebrews with eminent New Testament scholar,

Gerald Borchert. As we were studying a chapter on Jesus as the perfect sacrifice, Dr. Borchert looked up and announced, "I don't understand the cross! Do you? I don't get it! I don't know how it works." I was astonished and relieved at the same time. If a brilliant professor like him struggles, why should I be surprised if the cross is beyond my comprehension? But then again, I do not understand how electricity works. And for the life of me, I have never been able to figure out how a refrigerator makes things cold. Automatic transmissions are alien creatures to me. All I know is that somehow, they work, and I depend on them. The same is true for me when it comes to the cross. I do not need to understand it, just depend on it. Somehow Jesus has removed my sins from me.

Tim Keller notes that if a person wrecks his car, someone has to pay to get it fixed. It should be the transgressor or his insurance. But what if he is uninsured and broke? The car will never be fixed unless Keller takes it upon himself to do what is impossible for the offender. He pays for the damage that he did not cause. That is what Jesus did. On the cross Jesus stepped forward and said, "I will pay for their sins." It is as if he went into the prison and said, "I will take the sentence. I will endure years in the cell, the noise and chaos, the bad food, the threats, the beatings and even the electric chair so that they can walk out free."

Somehow, in a way that we can never fully explain or understand, that is what Jesus did. He took upon himself our sin and its penalty. We are therefore cleansed of our sin. We are forgiven and justified. In God's sight, it is as if we had never sinned.

By the cross of Christ we are rescued from the consequences of our sin. Jesus' death overcomes our estrangement with God. When Jesus died, the curtain in the Temple was torn in two, indicating that the way was now open to approach God. The barrier of sin has been removed. The cross also eliminates any sense of condemnation, for we know that Jesus has wiped the slate clean. "There is now no condemnation for those who are in Christ," is the way that Paul put it. Finally, the cross frees us from the ultimate consequence of a life lived outside of God's will which is hell. Jesus has paid the price to set us free.

Phase Two
Easter Sunday – The Resurrection

The second phase of the rescue mission took place on Easter Sunday with the resurrection of Jesus from the grave. Without the resurrection, Jesus' death is meaningless. It would mean that evil and Satan had won. The Good News is not only that Jesus died on the cross for our sins, but that he arose on the third day. The resurrection rescues us from the ultimate consequences of our sin – death.

What difference does that make? Anglican scholar N.T. Wright says that it makes all the difference in the world. If Jesus rose from the dead, it changes everything!

For one thing, it proclaims that a new age has dawned. Evil and death have been defeated. In former times Satan held the world in his clutches. Not anymore. God has invaded his territory. There is a new sheriff in town. A new power has been unleashed into the world. It is the greatest power the world has ever seen – the power to raise the dead back to life. If Jesus was raised from the dead, anything is possible. There is no problem too big for God to solve, no illness too grave for God to heal. In an interview Wright suggested that in this new age we avoid using the word "miracle" because by definition, a miracle is an abnormality. In this new resurrection age, miracles are the new normal.

Resurrection not only has significance for our lives now, but also in the future. Jesus declared that "I am the Resurrection and the Life. Whoever believes in me, though he dies, yet shall he live. And whoever lives and believes in me shall never die." (John 11:25) The curse of death has been broken. We will live on after death. The Apostle Paul wrote that Jesus' resurrection needs to be understood as the "first fruits" of an abundant harvest of future resurrections. As will be discussed in a later chapter, the ultimate Christian hope is that following heaven we will experience a bodily resurrection to live eternally on this redeemed and renewed earth.

I have conducted many funerals in my years as a pastor. Typically the most wrenching moment is the graveside committal service. This is when family and friends say their final goodbyes to their loved one as he or she is lowered into the ground. But I have come to see this practice as perhaps the most hopeful and comforting ritual we perform. I remind the mourners that Paul teaches us in I Corinthians 15 that our bodies are like seeds that are planted in the ground. One day these seeds will rise to new life. The grave is not a final resting spot. It is a garden where we plant a seed that will one day sprout into everlasting life!

In the resurrection of Jesus on Easter Sunday, God rescues us from the power of evil in this world and from death in the next.

Phase Three
Pentecost – The Gift of the Holy Spirit

The third phase of the rescue mission took place on Pentecost, fifty days after Easter. That was when the Holy Spirit was poured out on all believers.

What does the Holy Spirit do for us? There are many works of the Holy Spirit, far too many to discuss in a brief chapter like this. But one important gift is new power over our sin. The Holy Spirit empowers us to resist temptation. What good does it do to be forgiven of our sins if we keep on committing them? On our own, that is what will happen. One of the insidious strengths of sin is its ability to take hold of us. But the Holy Spirit breaks us free.

St. Augustine knew this by experience. The besetting sin of his life was lust. His addiction to sex prevented him from committing himself to Christ, long after he had been intellectually convinced of the truth of Christianity. He was powerless to resist. But one day he had an experience of the Holy Spirit that broke sin's hold on him. It is true that he was never completely free from lust. Indeed, he struggled with it for the rest of his life. But neither was he powerless anymore to resist.

In the hymn, "O for a Thousand Tongues to Sing," there is a line that reads, "He breaks the power of canceled sin, He sets the prisoner free." That is what the Holy Spirit does for us. Through Jesus' death on the cross our sins are cancelled. By the work of the Holy Spirit, the power of sin is broken, and we are now free not to sin.

Paul assures us that:

> *No temptation has seized you except what is common to man. And God is faithful; he will not let you be tempted beyond what you can bear. But when you are tempted, he will also provide a way out so that you can stand up under it.*
> (I Corinthians 10:13)

The book of Hebrews echoes this promise.

> *Because he himself suffered when he was tempted, he is able to help those who are being tempted...For we do not have a high*

priest who is unable to sympathize with our weaknesses, but we have one who has been tempted in every way, just as we are — yet was without sin. Let us then approach the throne of grace with confidence, so that we may receive mercy and find grace to help us in our time of need. (Hebrews 2:18, 4:15, 16)

In 2010 thirty-three miners were caught in a seemingly hopeless predicament. And yet the coordinated efforts of many people saved their lives. So it is with us. Two thousand years ago there was a spiritual rescue mission. All three persons of the Trinity had a hand in saving us. The Son saved us from punishment by dying on the cross. The Father defeated death by raising Jesus from the grave. The Holy Spirit set us free from the lure of temptation by pouring out his power on all believers. The victory has been won and the rescue mission has been a success.

For further reading:

Tim Keller, "The Prodigal God"

Discussion Guide

1. Ask the class to share an experience of being rescued from some danger or dilemma. What were their feelings?

2. Jesus' rescue mission included saving us from the consequences of our sin. What are some of those consequences? What do you think Hosea meant when he said, "They have sowed the wind and reaped the whirlwind?"

3. Discuss the difference between forgiveness and justification. Have the class come up with a list of some of the things Satan says to tempt or accuse. Read each one of them aloud and have the class

respond, "Liar!" What difference would it make if you knew in your heart that you were not just forgiven, but justified?

4. Invite the class to share an Easter memory. What made it such a special day? What is the message of Easter? Review the points in "Phase Two."

5. In some religious traditions, a person's cremated remains are thrown into the sky or sprinkled on the ground or ocean. What does that symbolize? How does it compare with the Christian tradition of burial? What is the message of burial?

6. What is the role of the Holy Spirit in our rescue? Does he magically remove temptation? What is our role?

Chapter Four

Our Response

My wife's grandfather was a men's hat-maker in Flint, Michigan. One of his regular customers was Charles Stewart Mott, a co-founder of General Motors and a man with more money than God. The two became fast friends. When Linda's father was in high school Mr. Mott offered him admittance and a full scholarship to attend General Motors Institute. G.M.I, now known as Kettering University, was an elite engineering school which guaranteed employment at General Motors upon graduation. Here was an opportunity that most only dreamed of. But he turned it down. He was having too much fun. He dropped out of school, joined the Navy and spent the next few years sowing wild oats. Only later did he realize his mistake. His youthful decision remained the regret of his life.

A promising new life was offered to him, but he turned his back on it because it asked of him something that he was not ready to give. To say "yes" meant that he would receive a priceless gift. It also meant a change in lifestyle, spending more time in the classroom and library and less playing drums or on the back of a motorcycle. That was a price he was not willing to pay.

This is analogous to the decision to become a Christian. The Gospel offers a new life of justification and forgiveness of sin, reconciliation with God, the indwelling of the Holy Spirit, victory over temptation and the assurance of Eternal Life in the New Heavens and New Earth. But in order to receive such gifts, God requires something of us, a response that many are reluctant to give. That is what we will look at in this chapter.

The gospel, which is what we have been looking at in the previous three chapters, calls for a response. We have a decision to make. We can choose to accept what God has done for us or we can refuse it. It is the decision about whether to become a Christian or not. It is a question of conversion.

Some might be thinking, "This is a chapter for someone else. I have been a Christian for many years. Why, I was baptized by Pastor Jones twenty years ago."

We dare not be so quick to assume that these pages do not apply to us. The church is plagued with a problem that some have dubbed "Nominal Christianity." This is the notion that being a Christian is merely a matter of mental assent to certain doctrines so that we will not go to hell when we die. Dallas Willard calls this the "gospel of sin-management." But being a Christian involves more than believing certain things. It is a whole lifestyle that includes entering into a vital relationship with Jesus and choosing to follow him in our day-to-day lives. Regrettably, many Christians are not aware of this. Billy Graham estimates that 90% of the people who came forward at his Crusades had already been baptized. And yet they never realized what it really meant to be a Christian.

What does conversion to Christ look like? It depends on who we ask. No two stories are identical. A "one-size-fits-all" pattern is non-existent. The Apostle Paul was converted instantly and dramatically on the road to Damascus. He saw a blinding flash of light and heard the audible voice of Jesus speaking to him. His was a spectacular conversion that took place in the blink of an eye. But for most people the journey takes longer. St. Augustine spent nine years wrestling both intellectually and spiritually until he surrendered. His experience is more typical. Methodist theologian George Hunter studied conversion in America and determined that the average believer took two and a half years to become a Christian. During that time they reported having approximately thirty encounters, each of which took them one step further down the road. These experiences included such things as an evangelistic sermon, a conversation with a believing friend, reading the biography of a Christian saint, etc.

Although there is no standard model to which we must all subscribe, there are three universal steps. They include:

- Reorienting Our Lives

- Trusting in What God has Done for Us

- Following Jesus as Lord of Our Lives

Reorienting Our Lives

The New Testament is filled with calls to repentance. John the Baptist warned, "Repent, for the Day of the Lord is coming!" Jesus declared, "Repent, for the Kingdom of God is near." At Peter's first sermon on the Day of Pentecost he said, "Repent, and be baptized."

But what is repentance?

We normally associate repentance with deep sorrow. It conjures up images of weeping, wailing, teeth gnashing, clothes rendering and ashes. Repentance can include any or all of these.

But the literal meaning of the Greek word repentance is "turning." To repent is to change direction or to choose a different road. Perhaps a good way to understand conversion is to envision it as reorienting the compass of our lives, away from self and towards God. Someone has described it as finding a new "center of gravity" for our lives.

As we discovered earlier in this study, the essence of sin is self-centeredness. We have usurped God's rightful place, pushing him off the throne of our lives. Adam and Eve's great sin was their desire to be like God. That is our primary sin as well. It might not be that we have rejected God outright, but we have kept him on the periphery.

A related problem is idolatry, which will be dealt with at length in a later chapter. Idolatry evokes images of bowing down to little statues. But it is more subtle than that. Idols are usually good things, such as health, family, a home, work, etc. They become idols when they are inordinately loved, that is, when we love them more than God.

The sins of self-centeredness and idolatry inevitably lead to destruction. Even those who do not profess to be Christian recognize this. The novelist David Foster Wallace delivered the commencement speech at Kenyon College in 2005, not long before taking his own life. In it he said this.

Everything in my own immediate experience supports my deep belief that I am the absolute center of the universe; the realest, most vivid and important person in existence. We rarely think about this sort of natural, basic self-centeredness because it's so socially repulsive. But it's pretty much the same for all of us. It is our default setting, hard wired into our boards at birth.

In the day-to-day trenches of adult life, there is actually no such thing as atheism. There is no such thing as not worshipping. Everybody worships. The only choice we get is what to worship. And the compelling reason for maybe choosing some sort of god or spiritual-type thing to worship — be it JC or Allah, be it YHWH or the Wiccan Mother Goddess, or the Four Noble Truths, or some inviolable set of ethical principles — is that pretty much everything else you worship will eat you alive. If you worship money and things, if they are where you tap real meaning in life, then you will never have enough, never feel you have enough. It's the truth. Worship your body and beauty and sexual allure and you will always feel ugly. And when time and age start showing, you will die a million deaths before they finally grieve you. Worship power, you will end up feeling weak and afraid, and you will need ever more power over others to numb you to your own fear. Worship your intellect, being seen as smart, you will end up feeling stupid, a fraud, always on the verge of being found out. But the insidious thing about these forms of worship is not that they're evil or sinful, it's that they're unconscious. They are default settings.[8]

Repentance is turning from these default settings of self-centeredness and idolatry and reorienting ourselves to a new North Star. It is starting down on a different road, much like the Prodigal Son as he set out on the way home. We might stumble and fall on the road. No doubt we will. But it doesn't matter, because at least we are on the right road and headed in the right direction. And when we trip, we can be sure that Someone will be there to pick us up, dust us off and set us on our way.

Trusting What God has Done for Us

The second step in conversion is learning to trust God. Some choose to use the word believe, accept or have faith. The word faith is near and dear to the heart of Protestants. "It is by faith alone that we are saved" was the clarion call of the Reformers. But what is faith?

Generally we think of faith as *believing* certain things about God and what he has done. This includes believing that God exists, that he created the world, and that he is All-powerful, All-knowing, and Everywhere-present. It also includes believing certain things about Jesus; that he was the Son of God who died on the cross for our sins, was raised on the third day, and ascended into heaven from where he will one day return.

---

[8] Quoted in Keller, Timothy. *Center Church: Doing Balanced, Gospel-Centered Ministry in Your City* (Grand Rapids: Zondervan, 2012) p. 34.

Believing what these doctrines affirm on the basis of biblical witness is essential, but it is just the beginning. As Flannery O'Conner said, "That's true, but it ain't true enough." After all, Satan believes all these things. He believes that God exists, and Jesus is his only Son who died on the cross for our sins. But that certainly does not make him a Christian.

Faith involves entering into a vital relationship with God. It is analogous to getting married. My wife and I have been married for four decades. What kind of relationship would we have if all I could say about her is that I believed in her, that is, that I believe that she exists and is a good person? I doubt that we would have celebrated many anniversaries!

Faith is having a trusting relationship with God. Trust is the basis of any healthy relationship. It means relying on God's goodness, kindness, compassion and help. It means believing he is with us and on our side. Above all, it means depending on the claim that he really did cover our sins through Jesus' death on the cross and that by raising him on the third day he secured victory over sin and death. Such a trusting relationship morphs into one of love and devotion.

Although faith is essential, it is not always easy. Trusting God is hard when there is bad news. Sometimes our lives are like a country-western song in which the crooner laments, "My dog died, my wife ran away, and my truck has a flat tire." It is tough to trust in God when our world falls apart – when our hearts are broken by betrayal, when there is a pink slip with our paycheck, or when the doctor announces that the results are positive. There are dark times in life when we can neither see God's hand nor feel God's presence. Faith is tough in those hours.

Abraham is regarded as the exemplary man of faith. But was it easy for Abraham to trust? Did he wake up every morning with a smile on his face in anticipation of what God was going to do? I doubt it. I am sure there were days when he cried out, "God, where are you? When are you going to fulfill your promises? I have been waiting for a son for decades now. Sarah and I are not getting any younger, you know." There were many times when Abraham complained, "How long, O Lord?"

It is not easy to hang on to faith. That is why Abraham was commended. He believed, even though the promise was long delayed, and he wrestled with questions and doubts. A person of faith will always be a mixture of trust and uncertainty, of confidence and doubt, of belief and unbelief. It is alright to question and doubt, as long as one's faith is just a nose length longer than one's unbelief. That will be enough.

Tim Keller offers a helpful illustration. Imagine two people preparing to board an airplane. One is confident and unafraid. She has complete faith in the aircraft, pilot and crew. She boards without a second thought. Another is petrified. He cannot imagine how such a large and heavy object could possibly become airborne. With much trepidation, he boards the plane. After an uneventful flight, both passengers safely reach their destination. Why? It was not the quality or quantity of their faith that mattered, but the competence of the pilot and equipment. In a similar manner, it is not the strength of our faith in God that matters, but his dependability and goodness. Even faith as small as a mustard seed is sufficient.

Following Jesus as Lord

The third step in conversion is choosing to follow Jesus as Lord. This is the most neglected aspect of the process. Dallas Willard wrote that "The Great Omission in American Christianity is the fulfillment of the command to make disciples, not just converts, as stated in Jesus

Great Commission."[9] He argues that being a Christian is not just a matter of believing certain things but living a certain way. That is as a follower of Jesus, which is the essence of discipleship. We are to follow both Jesus' teachings and example.

Willard further taught that Jesus is not a remote savior, waiting for us in heaven after we die. He is with us now as a leader and teacher to whom we apprentice ourselves. He shows us the best way to live. Discipleship is apprenticeship.

Of what does such apprenticeship consist?

> *"Most of evangelism today is obsessed with getting someone to make a decision: the apostles, however, were obsessed with making disciples."*
>
> ***Scot McKnight***

First of all it includes engaging in the kind of spiritual practices that Jesus did. It means imitating Jesus' example in what he did to nurture his spiritual life. This includes such things as solitude, prayer, worship, and scripture. These spiritual disciplines, which we will explore in detail in the next unit, will lead us to an even closer relationship with God as well as transform us into Christlikeness.

Secondly, it means living the kind of life that Jesus modeled. It is a life of virtue, compassion and service. Scot McKnight summarized this in something he calls "The Jesus Creed." When Jesus was questioned about the greatest commandment, he replied, "Love God with all your heart, mind and strength and your neighbor as yourself."

---

[9] Willard, Dallas. *The Spirit of the Disciplines: Understanding How God Changes Lives* (New York: HarperCollins, 1988) p. 15.

That's it. That is all there is to it. That is how a follower of Jesus will live. He or she will love God and love others.[10]

But it is impossible to live this way without first tending to our spiritual lives, i.e., the spiritual disciplines. To try to do so is as preposterous as if I decided, "I am going to play basketball like Michael Jordan." It cannot be done. The only way MJ was able to perform his magic on the court was because he first spent years in conditioning, study and practice.[11] The only way we can begin to live like Jesus is to engage in his spiritual practices. But if we do, little by little we will begin to resemble him.

The invitation of this chapter is to be converted. That involves the three steps of

Reorienting Your Life, Trusting in What God has Done for You, and Following Jesus as Lord. This is a call, not just to unbelievers, but also to those who sit in the pew every Sunday.

If only Linda's father had accepted C.S. Mott's offer. He would have had to make changes, but his life would have been different.

An even better offer is extended to us. It promises a richer life both now and in the world to come. If you are ready to respond, consider offering a prayer like this one, adapted from Tim Keller.

Father, even though I have always believed in you and Jesus, the truth is that my fundamental desire and trust has been in myself. I have lived my life on my own terms and have assumed that my goodness and decency were sufficient to save me. I have failed to realize how far I am away from you and how serious my sins have been. But I have also failed to recognize how deeply I am loved by you and how

---

[10] McKnight, Scot, *The Jesus Creed: Loving God, Loving Others* (Brewster, Massachusetts: Paraclete, 2004) *p. 11.*
[11] Willard, op.cit. pp. 3-5

much Jesus has done for me through his death and resurrection. And so, as far as I am able, I turn from my old life and reorient myself to you. I ask you to forgive me for my sins and give me the assurance that I have been forgiven. I put my trust in you and ask that you would receive and accept me, not for anything I have done but because of everything that Christ has done for me.

For further reading:

John Stott, "Basic Christianity"

Discussion Guide

1. Imagine sitting on the beach when an attractive member of the opposite sex sits down next to you. After a brief chat he (or she) announces. "I like you. In fact, I love you and want to spend my life with you. We will be very happy together. Will you marry me?" How would you react? What are some of the things you would want to consider before making such a commitment?

2. How does this compare with some evangelistic techniques? (If possible, have copies of the Four Spiritual Laws available.) Although many people have become Christian through such means, what are some potential problems with this approach?

3. What images does the word "repent" conjure up? Point out that the core meaning is to "turn" or "reorient" oneself to God. Is this a helpful concept? What are some of the things from which we need to turn? Is this something we can do on our own? What is the role of the Holy Spirit in this process?

4. Read the David Wallace quote. What do you think about his comment that we are hard-wired for self-centeredness? What do you think about his observation that we all worship something? What are the consequences of this?

5. What is the difference between "belief" and "trust"? Is it easy or difficult to trust God? Why or why not? What experiences have helped you to trust in God? Alternatively, what experiences have you or others had that make it difficult to trust in God?

6. Is trust based on subjective feelings or objective realities? What is the role of feelings for faith? (Note that in first chapter we discussed how God's love is better *seen* than *felt*.)

7. Are there Christians who have accepted Jesus as Savior, but not as Lord? What does it mean to be a Lord? What are some concrete examples of following Jesus in everyday life?

Chapter Five
The Whole Gospel

Bob Pierce was the founder of World Vision, a large evangelical relief organization. Earlier in his life he served as an evangelist who in 1948 led a Youth for Christ campaign to China. At his final sermon a little girl gave her life to Christ. When she told her parents about her decision, she was beaten, disowned and cast out. She found her way to a mission station where she was taken in. In the morning the director of the mission confronted Bob Pierce and demanded, "This little girl did what you told her to do and now she has lost everything. I am already sharing my rice bowl with six other children who have no homes, and I cannot take in even one more. The question is, what are you going to do? You created this problem, Mr. Pierce. Now what are you going to do about it?"

In Richard Stearns' book, "The Hole in the Gospel" he writes,

What are you going to do about it? That was the question that confronted Bob Pierce that day in 1948, when he met head-on with the desperate plight of one child. And in one moment he learned something groundbreaking about the gospel that he so freely preached: the whole gospel involves more than preaching; it also means caring about the whole person and finding ways to meet that individual's needs. When we look around our world and see children beaten and crying, huddling in their broken-down houses, aren't we confronted with the very same question that challenged Bob Pierce?[12]

Thus far in our study we have only heard part of the gospel. That is the individual, personal side of the message; that Jesus lived, died and rose to save us from our sins.

---

[12] Stearns, Richard *The Hole in the Gospel* (Nashville: Thomas Nelson, 2009) p.225

But the Gospel is bigger than that. Jesus' identity is larger than as our personal savior and his mission is greater than saving individual souls. He made that clear in his inaugural sermon at Nazareth.

The scroll of the prophet Isaiah was handed to him. Unrolling it, he found the place where it is written: "The Spirit of the Lord is on me, because he has anointed me to preach good news to the poor. He has sent me to proclaim freedom for the prisoners and recovery of sight for the blind, to release the oppressed, to proclaim the year of the Lord's favor." Then he rolled up the scroll, gave it back to the attendant and sat down. The eyes of everyone in the synagogue were fastened on him, and he began by saying to them, "Today this scripture is fulfilled in your hearing." (Luke 4:17-21)

"I believe the word gospel has been hijacked by what we believe about 'personal salvation,' and the gospel itself has been reshaped to facilitate making 'decisions.' The result of this hijacking is that the word gospel no longer means in our world what it originally meant to either Jesus or the apostles."

Scot McKnight

Jesus is King[13]

Notice what Jesus said about his identity. He claimed to be the Messiah, or "anointed one," for that is the literal translation of the word. Jesus announced that he was the one for whom Israel had long waited, the promised King who would sit on David's throne. By definition, a King is no mere personal savior and friend. He is ruler over a whole realm of peoples and lands. He is concerned with the well-being of every individual, along with the well-being of the whole nation.

---

[13] Credit for most of the content in this section is due to Scot McKnight's *The King Jesus Gospel*

Such kingship was the central understanding of Jesus in the apostolic age. In Peter's first sermon he announced, "God has made this Jesus, whom you crucified, both *Lord* and *Christ*." (Acts 2:36) Paul wrote that Jesus "was declared with power to be the Son of God by his resurrection from the dead: Jesus *Christ* our *Lord*." (Romans 1:4) His Lordship extends over all creation. "For by him all things were created: things in heaven and on earth, visible and invisible, whether thrones of powers or rulers or authorities, all things were created by him and for him." (Colossians 1:16) When we are tempted to think of Jesus' ministry in individual terms, we only need to remember that John 3:16 reads "God so loved the *world* that he gave his one and only Son."

Some years ago there was a popular little book entitled, "Your God is Too Small." It argued that we have inadequate images of God. Some common misconceptions are of God as a resident policeman, a doting grandfather or an emotionally distant parent. The author suggested that we need to enlarge our understanding of God. He is much more than what we envision. Perhaps a sequel with the title "Your Jesus is Too Small" is in order. He is more than just our personal friend and savior. He is King of Kings and Lord of Lords. That is what Jesus announced in his first sermon.

Notice also what Jesus intended to do. His Kingdom would bring a social revolution in which the poor would be fed, the imprisoned set free, the blind given sight and the oppressed released. It would be a kingdom marked by justice, righteousness and peace. His mother, Mary, foresaw this. In her song, called the "Magnificat," she sang, "He has brought down rulers from their thrones but has lifted up the humble. He has filled the hungry with good things but has sent the rich away empty." (Luke 1:52, 53)

In his first sermon Jesus said nothing about dying to be our personal savior. Instead he announced his kingship and mission to redeem the whole world. His inaugural address proclaimed the Kingdom of God. That is the other half of the Gospel message.

Our Role in Kingdom Building

This has implications for us. If we are followers of Jesus, we ought to be about the work and ministry he came to perform. We are to be engaged in the kind of work he conducted while on earth. But as long as we think of Jesus' mission in individualistic terms, we are not inclined to do much to help those who are in need. It is when we begin to grasp Jesus' global mission that we are inspired to rise up and join in the mission.

That is the primary way God gets things done. God builds his Kingdom through people. Theresa of Avila wrote, "God has no body on earth but yours, no hands but yours, no feet but yours. Yours are the eyes through which Christ's compassion for the world is to look out. Yours are the feet with which he is to go about doing good. And yours are the hands with which He is to bless us now." Former President Jimmy Carter understands that. He said, "My faith demands – this is not optional – my faith demands that I do whatever I can, wherever I can, whenever I can, for as long as I can with whatever I have to try to make a difference."

We all have a role to play. God has gifted and called each of us for some kind of service and ministry. There are tasks that will not be accomplished unless we do them.

Amazingly, the deeds we perform here on earth have eternal significance. As mentioned earlier, the Christian's ultimate hope is that Jesus will return and redeem *this world*. God created the world and declared it good. His plan is not to destroy it but transform it back to its original state. Our work for the Kingdom contributes to the redemption of this planet.

Anglican scholar, N.T. Wright described our role in God's plan this way:

What you do in the Lord is not in vain. You are not oiling the wheels of a machine that's about to roll over a cliff. You are not restoring a great painting that's shortly going to be thrown on the fire. You are not planting roses in a garden that's about to be dug up for a building site. You are – strange as it might seem, almost as hard to believe as the resurrection itself – accomplishing something that will become in due course part of God's new world. Every act of love, gratitude, and kindness; every work of art or music inspired by the love of God and delight in his creation; every minute spent teaching a severely handicapped child to read or to walk; every act of care and nurture, of comfort and support, for one's fellow human beings and for that matter one's fellow nonhuman creatures; and of course every prayer, all Spirit-led teaching, every deed that spreads the gospel, builds up the church, embraces and embodies holiness rather than corruption, and makes the name of Jesus honored into the world – all of this will find its way, through the resurrecting power of God, into the new creation that God will one day make.[14]

God uses changed people to change the world.

This presents us with the uncomfortable question that confronted Bob Pierce. What are we going to do? What, if anything, have we done as individuals or as a church to address the crying needs of the world? What can we do about poverty? Hunger? Homelessness? AIDS? Oppression?

The enormity of the needs can be overwhelming. The problems seem so great that we are tempted to throw up our hands in despair and

---

[14] Wright, N.T., *Surprised by Hope: Rethinking Heaven, the Resurrection, and the Mission of the Church* (New York: HarperCollins, 2008) p. 208.

say, "What is the use? How can one person possibly make a difference?"

But look at Jesus' example. When he inaugurated his kingdom, he did not run around doing big things. He did not march up to the halls of power in Jerusalem and Rome and throw down the gauntlet. He did not marshal an army to overthrow the oppressors. He did not even build a hospital or school. Jesus went around doing little things. He simply met the needs of the people around him. He befriended the outcasts, fed the hungry, taught the inquisitive, healed the sick and preached to those who came to hear. These are all relatively small deeds.

For most of us, all Jesus asks is that we do small things. That is a relief, since most of us are one talent servants. Few of us are equipped to make a big difference. In his last parable about the sheep and goats in Matthew 25, Jesus taught the centrality of small acts of kindness; visiting the sick and imprisoned, giving a cup of cool water to the thirsty, feeding the hungry and clothing the naked. But these are big in God's eyes, for as we do them, we are doing them as to Jesus. Even small acts of service have eternal significance.

In the conclusion of his Spiritual Exercises, Ignatius of Loyola described "The Call of the King." He asks us to imagine a great king who is about to launch a major campaign to free his realm of evil and oppression. The task will be hard and dangerous. He invites us to join him. If we do, we will suffer privations. There will be hard marching, miserable food, and cold nights spent sleeping on the ground. But there is also promised the thrill of being a part of a great cause and of sharing in the great victory. Will we join the king?

This is the question King Jesus poses to us.

For further reading:

Scot McKnight, "The King Jesus Gospel: The Original Good News Revisited"

Discussion Guide

1. Why do you think Jesus came? List the reasons

2. Read Jesus' first sermon as recorded in Luke 4:17-21. What did Jesus say were the reasons he came? How do the two lists compare?

3. How does God accomplish his will in the world? How much of it depends on using human instruments? Can you think of examples from the Bible? Today? What does this say to you?

4. How well do you think the church in general is doing in fulfilling Jesus' kingdom? What are some of the specific things your church is doing? On a scale of 1 – 10 how does your church rate?

5. What are some of the specific needs of your community? Is there any way that your church or you individually could help?

6. What do you see as your spiritual gift? How well are you exercising it? Can you think of one thing you can do to help?

7. What is the motivation for service? Is it possible for a Christian to be spiritual, but not actively involved in service? Is it possible for a Christian to be actively involved in service, but not in personal spiritual nurture? Can you think of examples? What is the connection between spirituality and service?

Section Two

Roadmap for the Journey –
The Spiritual Disciplines

Chapter Six
Introducing the Spiritual Disciplines

Some months ago I introduced the spiritual disciplines to my Sunday School class. I suggested that discipleship includes the practices of prayer, scripture study, contemplation and worship. These are the tools that God uses to transform us into Christlikeness.

Then Curtis raised his hand.

Ever the good-natured pot-stirrer, he asked, "Why should I want to do that? Why should I want to engage in these practices? They sound like a lot of work. And why should I want to become like Jesus? Things did not work out so well for him. He wound up on a cross. Neither the process nor the outcome is particularly appealing to me."

"And now, with God's help, I shall become myself."

Soren Kierkegaard

I thought he had me.

But then I remembered (thank you Holy Spirit) that Thomas Merton said, "For me to be a saint is to be *myself*."

I responded something like this. "The spiritual disciplines are not just designed to make you more and more like Jesus. They are also intended to help you become more and more yourself. That is, they are tools that will assist you in becoming your true and best self."

I continued, "A friend in the ministry, Bob Roberts, once told the story of an elderly woman who grasped his hands after the worship service and said, 'Bob, my prayer for you is that you might catch a glimpse of the wonderful person God dreamed you could be when he made you.'"

I went on to say, "The purpose of the disciplines is transformation. They help us become all we were meant to be – people of character, integrity, freedom, graciousness, strength, peace, and joy. They enable us to become individuals who actually live by the Sermon on the Mount - loving our enemies, forgiving those who hurt us, refraining from hurtful words, keeping our promises, sharing quietly with the needy, and living lives of moral purity. It is just a better way to live."

The spiritual disciplines are tools that God uses to help us know him and become more fully ourselves. That is God's desire for us. Paul wrote, "If anyone is in Christ, he is *a new creation.*" He did not say, "If anyone is in Christ he will go to heaven when he dies." His emphasis is on acquiring new life now. In Christ we become better people. In Galatians 5 Paul writes that we will become people whose lives are marked by love, joy, peace, patience, kindness, goodness, faithfulness, gentleness and self-control.

Jesus said something similar. "I came that you might have life, and that more abundantly." (John 10:10) He was not talking about going to heaven after we die but receiving new life here and now in this world. If we think that being a Christian is just a matter of believing certain things so that we will not go to hell when we die, we are missing out on one of the central purposes of Jesus' ministry.

Psychologist David Benner summarized it in this way, "Our true self-in-Christ is the only self that will support authenticity. It and it alone provides an identity that is eternal. Finding that unique self is… the problem on which all our existence, peace and happiness depend. Nothing is more important, for when we find our true self, we find God, and if we find God, we find our most authentic self…As we become more and more like Christ, we become more uniquely our own true self."[15]

Jesus came to give us new life. The question is, "How many of us are living it?" Too few, I am afraid. This new life sounds more like a dream than a reality. Many, perhaps most Christians are not experiencing it. That includes even some well-known leaders.

John Ortberg spoke for many of us when he wrote,

I am disappointed with myself. I have a nagging sense that all is not as it should be. Sometimes I am too concerned about what others think of me, I am disappointed for my life as a father, a husband, friend, neighbor, and human being in general. I am disappointed that I still love God so little and sin so much. Sometimes, although I am aware of how far I fall short, it doesn't even bother me very much. And I am disappointed at my lack of disappointment.[16]

Why is that? Why are we missing out on the new life? Why are we failing to be the people God created us to be?

Part of the answer is that we are not even aware that new life is possible. Because Christianity has been reduced to an insurance policy to protect us from hell, many people neither expect change in their own lives nor in those of other believers. It is common to hear expressions such as, "That is just the way I am, and you need to accept me" or "He is a stubborn old goat who will never change." This is patently false. Scripture teaches that we are to be transformed.

Another problem is that we are unclear about how transformation occurs. Some think it is automatic; that a mere profession of faith leads to new life. True, some people experience a radical change the

---

[15] Benner, David G. *The Gift of Being Yourself: The Sacred Call to Self-Discovery* (Downers Grove, Illinois: InterVarsity Press, 2015) p. 17.
[16] Ortberg, John. *The Life You've Always Wanted: Spiritual Disciplines for Ordinary People* (Grand Rapids: Zondervan, 1997) pp. 11-13.

moment they receive Christ, but they are the exceptions rather than the rule. For most it is a gradual process.

Transformation requires effort on our part. Although the Holy Spirit will do most of the heavy lifting, we must cooperate with him in the process. We do that by following Jesus' teachings and example, especially when it comes to spiritual practices. We will never become the new people God created us to be if we neglect these disciplines. The Holy Spirit will use them to bring us closer to God. In the disciplines we spend time with God. The time we spend helps us know God in a deeper and more personal way. He becomes our friend and is no longer a stranger or mere acquaintance.

"One of the primary laws of human life is that you become like what you worship"

N.T. Wright

This is the source of transformation. As we spend more time with Jesus, we gradually become more and more like him. Theologian G. K. Beale wrote a book entitled, "We Become What We Worship" in which he said, "What people revere, they resemble, either for ruin or restoration." The twelve that Jesus chose to be his in his band became disciples by living with Jesus; walking with him, talking with him, eating with him, and serving with him. That is the way disciples were made two thousand years ago. That is the way they are formed today.

Transformation is not a matter of willpower. It is not the result of effort, of trying hard to make it happen. We learn this truth from Alcoholics Anonymous. AA teaches that willpower and effort are not enough to break free from the bottle. It is only by working the Twelve Steps that one can overcome the addiction.

Dallas Willard said that "It is not a matter of trying, but of training."[17]
John Ortberg fleshed this out when he wrote,

For much of my life, when I heard messages about following Jesus, I thought in terms of trying hard to be like him. So after hearing (or preaching, for that matter) a sermon on patience on Sunday, I would wake up Monday morning determined to be a more patient person. Have you ever tried hard to be patient with a three-year-old? I have – and it generally didn't work any better than would my trying hard to run a marathon for which I had not trained. I would end up exhausted and defeated. Spiritual transformation is not a matter of trying harder, but of training wisely. Respecting the distinction between training and merely trying is the key to transformation in every aspect of life. For me, this truth brought light to the darkness. For the first time as an adult, I found the notion of following Jesus a real, concrete, tangible possibility. I could do it. Following Jesus simply means learning from him how to arrange my life around activities that enable me to live in the fruit of the Spirit. The traditional term for such activities is 'spiritual disciplines.'[18]

This is a gradual process. As we practice the disciplines, we might not see much progress, but something is happening. We are slowly becoming more like Jesus and our true and best selves. When a seed is planted in the ground there is no immediate sprout. But deep within the earth, hidden and unseen, life is beginning to churn. Similarly, in June the foliage of a maple tree is green. But come October the leaves are a riot of yellow, red and orange. The transformation is stunning, but no one saw it happen.

New Testament scholar N. T. Wright shares a story that illustrates how God performs this miracle.

---

[17] Willard, Dallas. *The Spirit of the Disciplines: Understanding How God Changes Lives* (New York: HarperCollins, 1988) p. 14.
[18] Ortberg, op.cit. pp. 43, 44.

I know a choir director who took on the running of a village church choir which hadn't had much help for years. They had struggled valiantly to sing the hymns, to give the congregation a bit of a lead, and on special occasions to try a simple anthem. But, frankly, the results weren't impressive. When the congregation thanked the singers, it was as much out of sympathy for their apparent hard work as out of any appreciation of a genuinely musical sound. However long they practiced, they didn't seem to get any better; they were probably merely reinforcing their existing bad habits. So when the new choir director arrived and took them on, gently finding out what they could and couldn't do, it was in a sense an act of grace. He didn't tell them they were rubbish, or shout at them to sing in tune. That wouldn't have done any good. It would have been simply depressing. He accepted them as they were and began to work with them. But the point of doing so was not so that they could carry on as before, only now with someone waving his arms in front of them. The point of his taking them on as they were was so that they could really learn to sing! And now, remarkably, they can. A friend of mine who went to that church just a few weeks ago reported that the choir had been transformed. Same people, new sound. Now when they practiced, they knew what they were doing, and thus they could learn how to sound better.

That is a picture of how God's grace works. God loves us as we are, as he finds us, which is (more or less) messy, muddy and singing out of tune…And the never-ending wonder at the heart of genuine Christian living is that God has come to meet us right there, in our confusion of pride and fear, of mess and muddle and downright rebelling and sin…But when we accept (God's grace) – when we welcome the new choir director into our ragged and out-of-tune moral singing – we find a new desire to read the music better, to understand what it's all about, to sense the harmonies, to feel the shape of the melody, to get the breathing and voice production right…and , bit by bit, to sing in tune.[19]

Our lives are pregnant with possibilities. We can experience new and abundant life. We can be changed persons who are more and more

---

[19] Wright, N.T. *After You Believe: Why Christian Character Matters* (New York: HarperCollings, 2010) pp. 62, 63.

like Jesus in word, deed and spirit. We can become our true and best selves, in all our uniqueness and beauty. The secret is the practice of the spiritual disciplines. It is to those that we now turn.

For further reading:

William A. Barry, "The Practice of Spiritual Direction"

Adele Ahlberg Calhoun, "Spiritual Disciplines Handbook: Practices that Transform Us"

Tim Muldoon, "The Ignatian Workout: Daily Spiritual Exercises for a Healthy Faith"

John Ortberg, "The Life You've Always Wanted: Spiritual Disciplines for Ordinary People"

Eugene H. Peterson, "A Long Obedience in the Same Direction: Discipleship in an Instant Society"

Dallas Willard, "The Spirit of the Disciplines: Understanding How God Changes Lives"

Discussion Guide

1. What health practices do you observe:

- Daily
- Weekly
- Monthly
- Yearly

2. Are there times when you do not feel like it? What do you do in those circumstances?

3. What is the purpose for these habits? What happens when you neglect them? (Be specific)

The Spiritual Disciplines have a similar function. They are intended to keep us spiritually healthy. By practicing them we grow closer to God. In the process we are gradually transformed into the likeness of Christ as well as our true and best selves.

4. What spiritual practices do you observe?

- Daily
- Weekly
- Monthly
- Yearly

5. Are there times when you do not feel like it? What do you do in those circumstances?

6. What are the consequences when you neglect them?

7. Which practices come easily and are enjoyable. With which ones do you struggle? Why do you think that is?

8. Dallas Willard recounts a time when he saw a bumper sticker that read, "Christians aren't different, just forgiven." What do you think of that slogan? How true is it? Is that OK? Why aren't Christians more different? *(Willard argues that it is because most are "nominal Christians" who think Christianity is merely a matter of believing certain things so that you will go to heaven. But we are called to be disciples, not mere believers. Discipleship includes practicing spiritual disciplines which lead to transformation.)*

9. What are some of the practices you associate with Spiritual Disciplines? (Examples might include prayer, worship, fasting…) The Disciplines that we will be exploring include:

- The Prayer of Examen
- Overcoming Desolations
- Hearing God
- Confession
- Scripture
- Spirituality in Everyday Life
- Church Life
- Stewardship
- Suffering

Are there any of these topics that hold special interest for you? What are they and why? Are there any that you would like to avoid? What are they and why?

10. Why are they called Disciplines? What does that suggest?

11. The Holy Spirit works through the Spiritual Disciplines to transform us into the likeness of Christ. What would becoming like Jesus look like?

12. The Spirit also uses the Disciplines to help us become our true selves. What would that look like?

Chapter Seven
The Prayer of Examen

In his book, "The Gift of Peace," Joseph Cardinal Bernardin related an incident that took place shortly after he had been named Bishop. In the course of get-acquainted visits he met with a group of seminarians with whom he lamented that the busyness of his position prevented him from having the kind of spiritual life that he desired. He was looking for their sympathy, but instead they challenged him. "Do you really mean it? Do you really want to develop a closer walk with the Lord? We can show you how." What could he say? He was trapped. He listened to their counsel and took it to heart. He wrote, "I was preaching a spirituality that I myself was not practicing." He resolved to give God the first hour of each day, a practice he continued for the rest of his life.[20]

The spiritual disciplines call for a similar commitment.

Where should we begin? What should we do first? The most logical place to start is with prayer. German theologian Dietrich Bonhoeffer said, "The prayer of the morning will determine the day."[21] A healthy prayer life is foundational for our spiritual well-being.

And yet this is where we often feel most inadequate. We do not know how to pray and clumsily stumble through. Our mind wanders, the monkeys start chattering, or we doze off to sleep. Our prayers lack form and substance, little more than a laundry list of the things we want God to do for us. And so we feel like failures.

If that describes you, be of good cheer; you are a member of a very large club. It is called the "Club of Those Who are Bad at Prayer."

---

[20] Bernardin, Joseph Cardinal. *The Gift of Peace* (New York: Doubleday, 1997) p. 5.
[21] Bonhoeffer, Dietrich. *Life Together* (New York: HarperCollins, 1954) p. 71.

Now you might be the President of the club, but you still have plenty of company. It includes such notables as Brother Lawrence who said, "I have always been poor at prayer. But when I accepted the fact that I would always be poor at prayer, things have gone much better for me." In a similar vein, Thomas Merton wrote, "We do not want to be beginners (at prayer). But let us be convinced of the fact that we will never be anything else but beginners all our life!"[22]

Many times our prayers seem to be little more than transactions. We put in our order, asking God to help us, heal us, guide us, protect us, fix us, etc. It is perfectly OK to present these concerns before the Lord, but what kind of conversation is that? It is like an interaction with the cashier at a fast food drive-up window. The content of our prayers reflects the quality of our relationship. What do we talk about with Jesus? What does this reveal?

If we struggle with prayer, it is not for lack of resources. Any Christian bookstore stacks dozens of books on prayer on its shelves. Online there are hundreds of titles. No doubt thousands of books have been written on the subject. But this only makes the task more daunting. Which model should we choose?

One form of prayer that millions of believers over the past five centuries have found helpful is called "The Examen" by Ignatius of Loyola. It is simple, clear and can be practiced by novices of any age. It takes about fifteen minutes. In this adaptation, there are four steps.

---

[22] Merton, Thomas. *Contemplative Prayer* (New York: Doubleday, 1969) p. 37.

Step One
Seek Illumination

In the first part of the Examen we pray for illumination. We ask that our eyes might be opened to see what God would have us to see. We pray that in the day ahead we might recognize him in the beauty of nature, in the pages of scripture, in things people say, in ideas that come into our minds and impressions that

"God desires to communicate with you all the time, but when you intentionally open yourself up to God's voice, you can often hear it more clearly."

James Martin

enter our hearts. We are praying that we might have the eyes of Jesus. In particular, we ask that we might see what God wants us to see as we go through the steps of the Examen.

God is far more present and involved in our lives than we could ever imagine. The Ignatian motto is, "Finding God in All Things." That is because God *can* be found in all things. But his activity is easy to miss. God is often subtle. He works in quiet, hidden ways. His hand is often clothed in everyday events and experiences. This means that if we are only looking for God in dramatic moments such as transcendent ecstasy or a miraculous rescue from a runaway train, most of God's dealings will escape us.

It is especially hard to see God's hand in the moment. At the time things are happening, it is almost impossible to recognize his presence and activity. His work is most easily seen in hindsight. The best way to see God in our lives is by looking in the rearview mirror.

This is what the Examen is designed to do. It is a prayer that focuses on yesterday. We pay attention to what happened in our lives during the previous twenty-four hours. Therefore, as we begin this prayer, we ask that our eyes be opened to see where God was active in our lives in the day before.

Try it! Take a few moments to pray that your eyes might be opened.

Step Two
Review Your Day: What Happened?

The next step is to mentally walk through the previous day, looking for God's goodness. Every day God sends gifts of love. In fact, the Bible tells us that every good thing was sent by God. "Every good and perfect gift comes from above." (James 1:17) In this step we extend our antennae and tune into yesterday's frequency.

God's gifts of love tend to be small, everyday events. That is why paying attention is so crucial. His blessings can be easily overlooked. As we review our day, we will see things that escaped us at the time.

Although this step calls for sensitivity to God's goodness during the day, not every day is infused with positives. We all have bad days when nothing seems to go right. That will be addressed later in this chapter and in the next. At present we are looking for God's blessings.

Imagine a young woman retracing her day. She recalls a conversation at the breakfast table with her husband. She sensed that he was troubled by something, and so she asked him what was wrong. She listened as he unburdened himself about a conflict with a colleague. Somehow, she was able to offer the right words of encouragement and counsel. He visibly brightened. She thanks God that he made her sensitive and used her to lift her husband's spirits. She then recalls her commute and the sunrise that painted the clouds orange. She thanks God for a glimpse of the wonder of creation and the reminder of his goodness and majesty. At the office, someone complimented her on a project she completed, a task that no one else could figure out. She thanks God for the ability and diligence to finish the job. In the evening her husband has prepared her favorite dinner and the two of them enjoyed and evening on the couch together. She thanks God for good food, a restful evening and a loving spouse.

These are the kind of small gifts for which we are to look.

We also pay special attention to "coincidences" and surprises that happen during the day. For example, suppose someone has been struggling with depression and "accidently" run across a magazine article about a new medication for his condition. Or a young woman has been questioning her career choice when out of the blue a friend says, "You know, I think you would be a great teacher." God speaks through these kinds of encounters. There are few true coincidences in a Christian's life. Our God loves to surprise us. More often than not, these are gifts from God's loving hand. We examine our day for coincidences and surprises. What is God saying or doing in them?

After my cancer diagnosis I was plagued with anxiety. The future looked misty at best, pitch black at worst. I prayed for some indication that I would be all right. A day or two later I went to visit a parishioner at the hospital. I always try to have an appropriate scripture passage prepared, but on this day I did not. I slipped into the chapel to select one. I had not been in there for over a year. After finding a passage I noticed an opened prayer book into which visitors had written their requests or offered their thanks. My eyes fell on these words. "This sickness is not unto death." (John 11:4) Of all the verses in the Bible, this was the one I needed the most. Was it a coincidence that I went into the chapel that day? Was it a coincidence that I noticed the book? Was it a coincidence that someone had written those words? I think not.

After noticing these daily gifts of love we give thanks. There is nothing that contributes more to a close relationship with God than gratitude. Spiritual directors advise that gratefulness is the portal to intimacy with God. When we recognize these good things as gifts from God and realize that they are signs of his love and goodness, we are drawn closer to him.

Gratitude not only brings us close to God but has a transforming effect on our lives. Disciples preacher Fred Craddock observed that:

Gratitude is the central virtue of the Christian life. There is no other virtue like gratitude – none. I've never known a person who was grateful who was, at the same time, mean or small or bitter or hurtful. Not when you're grateful. When our children were small, if an angel had come into the room and said, "Now you may receive one virtue, one quality for each child; what will it be?" I am sure my wife and I would discuss it, but I already know what my request would be. Make them always grateful.[23]

Try it! Take a few moments to review your day and give thanks to God for his gifts of love to you.

Step Three
Review Your Day: What Did You Feel?

In this third step we once again review our day. But this time we will do not look at what *happened* but what we *felt*. Every day we experience a cascade of different emotions. In this step we pay attention to what was going on inside of us yesterday. We walk through our previous twenty-four hours, noting the emotional highs and lows. We especially focus on heavy feelings such as worry, depression, guilt, anger and sadness.

---

[23] Craddock, Fred. *The Collected Sermons of Fred Craddock* (Louisville: Westminster, 2011) p. 31.

If the day was one of unqualified peace and contentment, give thanks to God and rest in his grace.

Chances are, however, that there were times when we felt low; perhaps burning with anger, green with envy or on the verge of tears in frustration or grief. Choose one or two of what Ignatius calls "Desolations," on which to focus. Something significant is happening in them.

Talk with Jesus about it. As the old hymn goes, "Take it to the Lord in prayer." Have an honest, heart to heart conversation with Jesus. For example, "Jesus, I do not know what is going on with me. I was carrying a lead ball of dread in my stomach all day. I am anxious about completing this project. In my head, I know I have the ability, but in my heart, I fear I will not measure up. There have been whispers about layoffs. I am so worried. And as a Christian I am troubled by my lack of faith and trust in you." As we pour out our hearts, we take time to be still and listen to what God is saying.

A conversation with God about our desolations will likely lead to one of the following kinds of prayer.

Confession

Perhaps the desolation is regret about something bad that we did; talking about a friend behind his back, snapping at the children or harboring evil thoughts about a co-worker. Unconfessed sin will eat away until it is resolved. As David wrote, "When I kept silent, my bones wasted away through my groaning all day long." (Psalm 32:3) But after David confessed, he experienced God's cleansing and healing forgiveness. He expressed his relief by writing, "Blessed is he whose transgressions are forgiven, whose sins are covered. (32:1)

Intercession

A prayer of intercession is one that is lifted up for someone else; perhaps a friend's diagnosis of cancer or a sister's divorce. In our sadness and faith we carry them to Jesus in prayer and lay them at his feet. Such prayers of intercession are commanded more than any other kind in the Bible.

Petition

This is the most common prayer to emerge from the Examen. It is a prayer for our own personal needs. We ask for comfort, healing, guidance or help with a problem. Such prayers make a difference! The Swiss theologian Karl Barth once said, "God does not just listen, he acts. And he does not act in the same way whether we pray or not. Our prayers exert an influence on God." In a similar vein, Archbishop of Canterbury Temple observed, "When I pray, coincidences happen. When I do not pray, coincidences do not happen."

Try it! Take a few moments to review your day, taking note of the heavy feelings you experienced, and then talk to Jesus about them.

Step Four
Looking Ahead

The fourth step calls for a change of focus. Instead of looking back, we now look forward to the day ahead. We do so with confidence and hope, thanking God for his forgiveness and for a new day in which to live. We profess our faith that he is with us, hears and answers our prayers, and will help us with the challenges ahead. Conclude by reciting the Lord's Prayer and then sit quietly in the Lord's presence – simply enjoying his company.

Try it! Take a few moments to look towards the day ahead.

The Prayer of Examen takes about fifteen minutes. But it makes a difference, even if done poorly. As Trappist monk Thomas Merton said, "Wanting to please God is in itself pleasing to God."

The story is told of one of the third century Desert Fathers who went out into the Egyptian desert to dedicate his life to God. He lived a life of faithful service through prayer and material simplicity. To ensure solitude, he located his cell miles from the nearest water. Every day he had to make the long trek there and back. As he grew elderly his heart tired of the service. The long walk for water became a symbol of his weariness at his solitary life. So much of his old nature still lingered. His prayer life no longer satisfied. He began to consider relocating and even quitting his vocation. "Why should I continue to do this?" he wondered. "I might as well move so that at least I can live closer to the water." As he spoke, he turned to see someone following him, counting his footprints. "Who are you?" the old man demanded. "I am an angel of the Lord, and I have been sent to count the footsteps of your faithfulness and give you your reward." When the monk heard this, his heart was lifted. He decided to move his cell even farther from the water.[24]

Even if we fail in our efforts to pray the Examen, it is comforting to know that there is One who is counting the footprints of our faithfulness and that a reward awaits us.

For further reading:

Fleming, David L. "What is Ignatian Spirituality?"

Timothy Gallagher," The Examen Prayer"

---

[24] Gallagher, Timothy. *The Examen Prayer: Ignatian Wisdom for Our Lives Today* (New York: Crossroad, 2006) pp. 139, 140

Discussion Guide

1. Play a few rounds of "I Spy." In this game someone says, "I spy with my little eye something green." Each of the participants is given a chance to guess until there is a winner.

2. In his book, "Letters to Malcolm" C.S. Lewis wrote, "We may ignore, but we can nowhere evade, the presence of God. The world is crowded with him. He walks everywhere incognito." There is a hiddenness to God's activity. This means that we must pay attention to where he might be speaking or acting in our lives. Much of the Prayer of Examen is devoted to playing "I Spy," looking for these footprints of God.

3. Explain that the Prayer of Examen, which was developed by Ignatius of Loyola five hundred years ago, has four steps.

- Pray for illumination
- Review yesterday, looking for God's gifts of love
- Review yesterday, paying attention to feelings
- Looking ahead and resting in God's presence

4. Lead the group in a prayer for illumination, asking that God might open everyone's eyes to see what he wants them to see.

5. Explain that the next step is to examine their previous day, looking for examples of God's goodness. These tend to be small gifts such as a good meal, meaningful conversation with a friend, a funny joke, etc. Invite them to retire to a quiet place for ten or fifteen minutes. Use this time to walk through their previous twenty-four hours, playing "I Spy" for God's blessings.

6. Regroup and ask questions such as:

- What happened? Were you able to identify gifts of love that went unrecognized at the time?
- What were they?
- What feelings did these evoke? Did it awaken gratitude to God?
- How did this exercise impact your feelings of/about God?

7. The next step in the Examen is to once again review the day, but this time paying attention to emotions. What feelings emerged? Were there low or heavy times? Pay particular attention to "desolations" such as depression, guilt, anxiety or stress. Have a conversation with God about this. Invite the group to return to their quiet places for ten or fifteen minutes to go through this exercise.

8. Regroup and ask questions such as:

- How did it go? Were you able to identify a variety of emotions?
- Were you able to talk to God about some of your heaviness?
- What was God like as you talked with him?
- Did you experience any comfort or guidance from him?

9. Invite the group to join you in a few moments of resting in God. It is not necessary to talk with God, but to just sit quietly with him. Conclude by reciting the Lord's Prayer and thanking God that he has given you a new day to enjoy and serve.

Chapter Eight
Overcoming Desolations

The first two months following my diagnosis of cancer were rough. I vividly recall feeling strapped into a roller coaster that I could not escape. I was plagued by insomnia and nightmares. Every afternoon dark clouds of depression rolled in. The heaviness was palpable and only relieved when I picked up my wife, Linda, from the train station at 5:30. Just sitting, talking and holding her were the best tonics. I had few coping skills for the anxiety that had become my constant companion.

In time, my spirits improved. After about ten weeks the weight began to lift. Part of this was due to the passage of time. I grew accustomed to my condition and gradually accepted my "new normal." The larger explanation was that I discovered Ignatius of Loyola, the 16th century founder of the Jesuits, and his reflections on Desolations. He not only taught me how to recognize the evil spirits of Desolation, but how to combat and overcome them.

What are Desolations?

St. Ignatius described Desolation as, "…darkness of the soul, disturbances in it, movement to low and earthly things, disquiet from various agitations and temptations, moving to a lack of confidence, without hope, without love, finding oneself totally slothful, tepid, sad, and, as if separated from one's Creator and Lord." It is heaviness of spirit that instills sadness and depletes energy for living.[25]   Desolation is the experience of weighty darkness and inner turmoil that can last for a brief or extended time.

---

[25] Gallagher, Timothy M. *The Discernment of Spirits: An Ignatian Guide for Everyday Living* (New York: Crossroad Publishing, 2005) p. 60.

Ignatius characterized such feelings and their causes as "evil spirits." What makes them evil is that they pull us away from God. Most of us can testify to the truth of this claim. In times of Desolation we have little interest or energy for the things of God. Worship, prayer and scripture hold small appeal. God seems distant, silent or absent. Our inclination is to avoid him, rather than seek him out. If not addressed, these evil spirits can lead us farther away from the only one who truly loves us and brings wholeness of life.

We need weapons to combat the evil spirits of Desolation. Jesuit priest Fr. Timothy Gallagher provides such artillery. In "The Discernment of Spirits" he offered three steps to overcome Desolations. These are:

- Notice the Desolations
- Understand the Desolations
- Take Action Against the Desolations[26]

Step One
Notice the Desolations

Consider the story of Sally. She has been experiencing low level anxiety for the past few days. She is burdened by the sense that something is not right. The feeling is subtle, so she ignores it and soldiers on. But one morning as she is spending a quiet hour in silence and prayer, she becomes aware of how strong and persistent is her disquiet. She is not sure where it is coming from but resolves to listen to what it is saying.

The first step is to be sensitive to when Desolations such as these come over us. The previous chapter on the Prayer of Examen included a section on paying attention to heavy feelings that we

---

[26] Ibid., p. 17.

experience during the day. Sometimes these Desolations are fleeting. The Desolations that most concerned Ignatius were those that persisted. The reason we need to be alert to these feelings is because Desolation is the *primary* way the Enemy attacks believers in Christ. This is quite distinct from the way Satan deals with non-Christians.

The main weapon that the Enemy wields to attack the non-believer is temptation. He attempts to entice his victim to do what is wrong. He does so by pointing out how attractive, pleasant and enjoyable the sin will be. He whispers how deserving his charge is and assures him that there will be no consequences.

Satan used this technique in the Garden of Eden. The serpent tantalized Eve by pointing out the loveliness and desirability of the forbidden fruit. He then cast aspersions on God's intent, suggesting the reason for the prohibition was God's jealousy. He wanted to keep all power for himself. Finally, Satan promised that Adam and Eve would suffer no penalty for their transgressions. They would actually be much happier, for in the end they would be like gods.

Once we succumb to temptation, the Evil One uses our sin against us. The word "Satan" means "Accuser." That is who he is; the Great Accuser. His method is to accuse us of being no better than the worst thing we have ever done. He tells us that our wrong deeds define our identity. If we ever lied, we are nothing but liars. If we ever cheated, we are nothing but cheats. If we ever failed, we are nothing but failures. His goal is making us feel condemned, ashamed and worthless. He tells us that God could never love or forgive people like us. His whole intent is to pull us away from God.

The devil adapts different tactics for the Christian. He no longer relies so heavily on temptation for he knows this is no longer as effective. The Christian has reoriented his or her life towards God.

With the Holy Spirit's empowerment, we are no longer as susceptible to the Evil One's wooing. The Spirit helps us to resist temptation.

Instead the Enemy uses what I call "The Five 'D's" of Desolation to trip us up. These are heavy, negative feelings that bring us down and pull us away from God. They include:

- Discouragement
- Depression
- Doubt
- Dread
- Distraction

This is not an exhaustive list of all the weapons in Satan's arsenal. But these are his preferred techniques.

Discouragement

This might be Satan's favorite weapon. He sends discouragement into our lives. It might be about our health, marriage, parenting, career or any number of vulnerable spots. He is especially keen to make us feel discouraged about our spirituality. He gleefully points out our failures and how far short we fall in our Christian walk. His purpose is to persuade us to abandon our quest of following Jesus.

Depression

Depression is Discouragement's cousin. Whereas discouragement might only stay for a visit, depression moves right in, plops himself down in the living room sofa, and shows no interest in ever leaving. Long time discouragement paves the way for deep seated depression. It is an effective tool, given the vast number of Americans who struggle with this condition.

Doubt

There are times when we can neither see God's hand nor feel God's presence. Satan capitalizes on these moments. He encourages us to question and doubt God's presence, goodness, wisdom, power and care. He seeks to undermine the faith and trust we have in the Lord by suggesting, "If God were really loving and true, you would not be going through something like this."

Dread

There are many threats and dangers in this fallen world. It is understandable that we are occasionally anxious and afraid. Satan fans the flames of our fears, telling us we will never make it, that all is lost. He sends dark clouds over our minds and hearts and urges us to live in a constant state of worry. Pastor/theologian Tim Keller wrote, "Worry is believing God will not get it right. Bitterness is believing that God got it wrong."

Distraction

It is not necessary for Satan to make us feel bad to accomplish his ends. Sometimes it is enough to distract us from what we should be doing. He seeks to pull us away from our prayers or

*"The lie of spiritual desolation includes a false equation between what the person **feels** in desolation and what the person **is** spiritually. If we accept this lie, discouragement and decline in progress toward God are not far away. If, however, we understand that such feelings indicated rather the trial of spiritual desolation, that God's call is to be faithful and thus grow spiritually through the trial, then an energizing liberation takes place in our hearts. The bonds of the lie are broken, and we are set free to follow the Lord with courage."*

Timothy M. Gallagher

mission by interrupting or enticing us. He encourages laziness and a wandering mind. We see him in action with Jesus in the wilderness. Satan sought to distract Jesus from his ministry by inviting him to turn stones into bread, to throw himself off the pinnacle or to bow down and worship him.

Step Two
Understand the Desolations

After noticing Discouragement, Depression, Dread, Doubt or Distraction our next step is to try to understand them. We ask ourselves, "Where are these feelings coming from? Why do I feel so anxious? Why am I so depressed?"

A few years ago our church sponsored an all-day spiritual retreat. At the end of the final session the retreat director handed out evaluation forms. She confessed that she once dreaded this process. A dozen participants could give her superlatives, but if one person was critical, she was crushed. She was puzzled by this Desolation and began to probe for understanding. She soon realized that it all stemmed from her childhood. As a girl, she had a big sister who was the princess of the family and the school. She was pretty, talented, bright and popular. Our director developed a sense of inadequacy. Her father reinforced these feelings. By word and deed he communicated that she would never measure up. All her life she carried this message. And so, when she received critical evaluations, she heard her father's voice telling her, "See? You will never be good enough." Once she understood where these dark feelings came from, she could take action against them. As she talked with Jesus about her pain, she heard his voice say, "You are my beloved child. You are good enough."

I was born with a streak of melancholy. It does not take much for me to become discouraged. Winston Churchill called depression the "black dog" that visited him regularly. This canine has apparently found my address because he periodically comes to pay me a call. When it does, it my task is to understand it. Typically the reason is that I have failed in some way. Perhaps the sermon was not up to par or a parishioner was upset with me. At times like that I need to examine myself to find the source of my bleak mood. It is almost always because I have forgotten my true identity. I allowed externals such as success or approval to determine my sense of well-being. I remind myself that my worth is not dependent upon what others think of me, but on what God does. I remember that my true identity is as God's beloved child. When I recall this, the sting of failure and rejection are lessened. They do not vanish, but neither do they devastate.

In step two we seek to understand the source of our Desolation

Step Three
Take Action against the Desolation

Once we understand the source of our Desolation, we can combat it. Our temptation is to do nothing, but to lie around and wait for the feelings to pass. This is a mistake. Ignatius taught how crucial it is for us to take action in order to break Desolation's hold. He provided guidance on how to do this.

There are five steps in the process.

1. Make no change in spiritual practices

When we are struggling with heavy feelings, our inclination is to quit our spiritual practices until we feel better. "I'll read my Bible later…I don't feel like praying right now…I think I will skip church today." This is a mistake. Ignatius counseled to never give up on prayers, Bible reading or weekly worship. We are to continue to do so, even if we do not feel like it. This is the most important step in breaking the power of the heaviness in our lives. The same principle applies to heart surgery patients. Within hours of the operation nurses will force them to get out of bed and walk. It is the last thing any patient wants to do, but experience has demonstrated that this is the quickest road to recovery.

2. Pray for God's supernatural power to help

The next step is to ask for God's help. Prayer changes things. Our prayers make a difference in how God works in our lives. Scripture tells us that God is Almighty. He is able to do anything. Let us avail ourselves of this power saying, "Lord, I am so fearful. Please break the power of this heaviness in my life." In my experience, the lifting is seldom instantaneous. But later in the day I always notice a difference.

3. Meditate on the promises of scripture

The Bible is a wonderful resource for times of Desolation. We are encouraged to meditate on passages of scripture that speak to the source of our discomfort. For example, if we are wrestling with anxiety, turn to Psalm 23 and read it slowly over and over. We allow its message of reassurance to comfort us. This is a strong argument for Bible Study. Even if scripture does not speak to us at the time of our study, we are pouring water into the well from which we will one day draw and drink. For those who struggle to find appropriate verses, the American Bible Society and the Gideons have web sites that offer suggestions.

4. Remember God's deliverance in the past

We not only remember the promises of God in scripture, but also the ways he worked in our lives in the past. We review our lives and contemplate the many times God has been there. Some people have been rescued from a serious accident or illness. Others have been delivered from trouble or have had doors open that proved to be great blessings. The God who was with us in the past is with us now.

5. Take suitable action

When Desolation comes to set up housekeeping, we feel like drawing the curtains, crawling into bed, and pulling the covers over our heads. That is OK for a while, but the danger is that we can get stuck. There comes a point when we need to get up and take action, often times doing the opposite of what we feel. This action usually involves some physical activity. It might be taking a walk or going shopping. It could include writing a note or extending an apology. One of the most valuable ways to come out of the funk is to find someone in need and serve him or her.

Our Enemy is real and destructive. He effectively uses "The Five 'D's'" to our detriment. But Satan is essentially a weakling and a coward. We must remember this. He is no match for the power of God. Scripture tells us that if we resist the Devil, he will flee!

Why are you downcast, O my soul? Why so disturbed within me? Put your hope in God, for I will yet praise him, my Savior and my God.

(Psalm 42:5)

For further reading:

Timothy M. Gallagher, OMV. "The Discernment of Spirits"

Timothy M. Gallagher, OMV. "Spiritual Consolation: An Ignatian Guide for the Greater Discernment of Spirits"

George W. Traub, SJ. "An Ignatian Spirituality Reader"

Discussion Guide

1. Read this story.

Alice is a dedicated woman of faith, active for years in her church. Sharing the life of the parish is a source of spiritual strength for her and brings her joy in the Lord. Of late, however, she no longer finds her participation to be life-giving. She begins to question her involvement. Alice sees herself as a pretty complete failure and feels altogether discouraged. She feels an emptiness of abandonment by God. She senses that God is no longer near, and she is overwhelmed with frustration. She wonders if she isn't losing her faith. All seems hopeless and meaningless.[27]

- Can you identify with Alice's story? If appropriate, share with the group.

- Break into small groups. Imagine Alice came to you and poured out her story. What would you do or say? What counsel would you offer?

2. The first step in overcoming Desolations is to notice them. Many times people choose to ignore these vague feelings. Ask the group to quietly review their last twenty-four hours, looking for heavy, disquieting feelings. Or invite them to pay attention to any persistent negative feelings. Ask everyone to write down one or two of these feelings and anonymously put them in a basket. If the group is comfortable with the idea, read the slips of paper and write them on the board. How many of them fall into the categories of Discouragement, Depression, Doubt, Dread or Distraction? Ask them what effect these feelings had on their spiritual lives. Remind them that these are the primary weapons the Evil One uses to pull believers away from God.

---

[27] Ibid., p. 58, 59

3. The next step is to understand the source of these desolations. Where are they coming from? Invite the group to find quiet corners where they can reflect on this question for ten minutes. Ask them to anonymously write down their discoveries and put them into a basket. If appropriate and with their permission, read these aloud.

4. The third step is to take action against these Desolations. This includes:

- Making no change in one's spiritual practices

- Praying for God's supernatural power to break the hold of the Desolation

- Remembering the promises of God

- Remembering how God has delivered in the past

- Taking some kind of physical action

As a group they will be focusing on the second and third bullets. Distribute a handout from the Gideons or American Bible Society of Biblical resources for times of trouble. Invite them to return to their quiet corner, first praying for God's deliverance and then reflecting on one of the Biblical promises. Read these slowly, over and over. Pay attention to a word or phrase that jumps out. Meditate on that.

5. Return and invite people to share their experiences. Remind them that sometimes the comfort or release comes later in the day.

6. Build a fire in the fireplace or out of doors. Burn the slips of paper and offer a prayer that in a similar way God would consume and destroy their Desolations. Alternatively, if the group has chosen not

to share their slips of paper, have each participant put them in the fire.

Chapter Nine

Hearing God

In the previous two chapters we focused on talking to God in prayer. But prayer, like all conversation, is a two-way street. We not only speak, we listen. This chapter will concentrate on hearing God.

Hearing God is more difficult than talking to God. It is easy to pour out our complaints, requests and thanks. But listening is another story. Many people complain that they have never heard God speak to them. Why is that?

The story is told of an elderly couple who had difficulty communicating with one other. The husband was convinced his wife was going deaf, so he tried an experiment. As she sat knitting across the room with her back to him, the husband said, "Mable, can you hear me?" No response. So he moved to the center of the room and asked again, "Mable, can you hear me?" Again, no response. Then he crept right in back of her and said, "Mable, can you hear me?" This time she turned around and announced, "Oh for heaven's sake, George. For the third time – yes, I can hear you."

> *"God whispers rather than shouts."*
>
> *Fred Craddock*

The problem is not that God is failing to speak. It is that we are having trouble hearing.

A major reason we do not hear God is that we are listening on the wrong channel. When we think of God speaking, we often imagine an audible voice from heaven. Sometimes God speaks in this way, but not often. God broadcasts on many channels. If we are only listening to one, we will miss him. It is necessary that we go up and down the dial with our ears tuned to his voice.

So how does God speak? The prophet Elijah discovered that it was in a "still, small voice." God was not heard in big, dramatic phenomena such as an earthquake, tornado or fire, but in quietness.

Of course, the clearest and most reliable way that God speaks is through the pages of scripture. The Bible is God's Word and in Chapter Eleven we will explore ways that we can hear a personal message through it. The focus of this chapter, however, is on the other ways that God speaks.

Dallas Willard, who authored the book "Hearing God," observed that the still, small voice generally takes three forms. They include:

- People
- Circumstances, especially coincidences and surprises
- Ideas of the mind and impressions upon the heart[28]

People

God often uses people as his mouthpiece. That was certainly true in Biblical days. God said to Moses, "You will be my spokesman." In the Old Testament God spoke directly to the prophets who then announced, "Thus saith the Lord…" Paul acknowledged that his words were not his own but were from the Spirit of God. When Jesus opened his mouth, it was the voice of God that was heard. Can anyone doubt that God spoke through these individuals?

God continues to speak through people. Those people include the following.

Preachers – The sermon is the proclaimed Word of God. Ideally, the congregation hears the voice of God in it. That should cause

---

[28]Willard, Dallas. *Hearing God: Developing a Conversational Relationship with God* (Downers Grove, Illinois: InterVarsity Press, 1999) pp. 95-102, 199.

every preacher to tremble. A graduating seminarian asked Swiss theologian Karl Barth, "What should I preach on my first Sunday?" Barth replied, "The question is not 'What shall you preach?' but 'How dare you preach?' Who do you think you are, presuming that you speak for God?" Whew! That is a challenge to all preachers. And yet God uses faithful and even unfaithful pastors to say what he wants to be heard. After all, God spoke through Balaam's ass. He still uses donkeys to get his message across.

Teachers – God speaks through all kinds of instructors, whether they are Sunday School teachers, college and seminary professors, or individual tutors. It is no accident that Jesus was called "Rabbi" which means "Teacher." God spoke to me through a professor who changed my life. In college I wrestled with my faith. Much about my fundamentalist upbringing confused and troubled me. But then I took a class from a New Testament scholar. I felt the clouds part as he opened up a new way for me to interpret scripture and express my faith. God spoke to me through him.

Mature Christians – God uses mature believers to give counsel to those who are struggling. A Christian therapist, spiritual director, or fellow believer can be the means by which the Lord speaks. Whenever I meet someone for counseling, I pray "Lord, help me to listen, to understand and then to say the right thing for this person." He always comes through, using me in ways I could never imagine.

Writers – How many people's lives have been changed by a book? Mine has. In the last few years God has spoken to me through the writings of Augustine, Francis of Assisi, St. Benedict, Ignatius of Loyola, Dietrich Bonhoeffer, Dallas Willard, Scot McKnight, and N.T. Wright.

Chance conversations – Sometimes God speaks in indirect ways. A casual remark, an overheard conversation, or something said in passing might actually contain a message for you. A famous author was asked how she chose her profession. She answered, "In high school a teacher wrote on one of my papers, 'This is good writing.' It was a small comment, but it changed my life. It was at that moment when I began to think I might have a career as a writer."

It is important to pay attention to what people say. Their advice, suggestions and encouragement might have a divine source. This includes criticism. St. Augustine's mother, Monica, loved to drink wine – evidently too much. One day she overheard her servant say to another, "Our mistress is nothing but a wine swiller." It cut Monica to the heart. In those words she heard the correcting voice of God spoken through someone who was neither a believer nor a friend.

Circumstances

The second way that God speaks in a "still, small voice" is through circumstances, various things that happen to us during the day. This is especially true of coincidences and surprises.

It is a central tenet of Biblical theology that God is a God of history. That means that he is actively involved in our world and speaks through this activity. God spoke through the Exodus, revealing his abhorrence of slavery by delivering the Israelites of their oppression. He spoke through the subsequent forty years of Wilderness Wanderings, teaching the Israelites about his provision and his insistence on holy living. He spoke through the Israelite's miraculous Conquest of the Promised Land, proclaiming his mighty power. Hundreds of years later he spoke through the Israelite's Exile to Babylon, revealing that he is a God of judgment. Forty years later spoke through the Jew's return to their homeland in Israel, demonstrating his forgiveness and resurrection power.

Since God speaks through events that are happening all around us, we would be wise to pay attention. The novelist and Presbyterian minister, Frederick Buechner, is an apostle for paying attention. In his book, "Listening to Your Life" he wrote,

I discovered that if you really keep your eye peeled to it and your ears open, if you really pay attention to it, even such a limited and limiting life as the one I was living opened up onto extraordinary vistas. Taking your children to school and kissing your wife goodbye. Eating lunch with a friend. Trying to do a decent day's work. Hearing the rain patter against the window. There is no event so commonplace, but that God is present within it, always hiddenly, always leaving you room to recognize him or not to recognize him. If I were called upon to state in a few words the essence of everything I was trying to say both as a novelist and as a preacher, it would be something like this: Listen to your life. See it for the fathomless mystery that it is. In the boredom and pain of it no less than in the excitement and gladness, touch, taste, smell your way to the holy and hidden heart of it because in the last analysis all moments are key moments, and life itself is grace.[29]

These words grew out of an experience in the darkest period of his life. His teenage daughter was anorexic, and all treatment had failed. Buechner felt desperately frightened and helpless. There was nothing he could do. He took a walk through his small Vermont hometown when he spotted a license plate that read, "TRUST." There was no word in the English language that he needed to hear more. It was the voice of God. A skeptic would sniff that it was a coincidence. But the eyes of faith see something else. Indeed, one God's favorite ways of speaking is through so-called "coincidences" and "surprises." Pay attention to them!

---

[29] Buechner, Frederick. *Listening to Your Life: Daily Meditations with Frederick Buechner* (New York: HarperCollins, 1992) p. 2.

God also speaks through pain and suffering. C.S. Lewis said that suffering is "God's megaphone." Although God talks to us in many ways, he shouts to us in our pain. When we encounter such times, it is prudent to ask, "What do you want me to know in this? What do I need to understand or change?"

James Dobson offers some practical advice on how to hear God. Whenever he needed to know God's will and how to proceed, he would pray, "Lord, I need to know what you want me to do, and I am listening. Please speak to me through my friends, books, magazines and circumstances."[30] Without fail, God answered within 24 – 72 hours.

Dallas Willard offered similar guidance.

Personally I find it works best if after I ask for God to speak to me in this way, I devote the next hour or so to some kind of activity that neither engrosses my attention with other things nor allows me to be intensely focused on the matter in question. Housework, gardening, driving about on errands or paying bills will generally do. I have learned not to worry about whether or not this is going to work. I know that it does not have to work, but I am sure it will work if God has something, he really wants me to know or do. This is ultimately because I am sure of how great and good, he is.[31]

The Lord will do the same for you.

Ideas and Impressions

So far, we have looked at ways that God speaks to us externally through people and circumstances. But God's "still, small voice" is also an internal phenomenon. It includes ideas that enter our minds and impressions that are laid on our hearts.

---

[30] Willard. op.cit. p. 199.
[31] Ibid. pp. 199, 200.

Sometimes God speaks through ideas that pop into our heads. John Ortberg tells of an experience when he woke up in the middle of the night. He looked over at his wife and felt overwhelmed by an intense sense of love. Scene after scene of their life together flashed in front of his eyes. He thought about how empty his life would be without her. For a long time he just watched his wife in wonder. It was one of the tenderest moments of his life. Then an idea came to him. He wrote,

Then something else happened that I did not expect. Propped up on one elbow and watching Nancy sleep, I thought, "While I lie in bed sleeping, God is watching me." And the thought came to me that God was saying something like this: "I love you like that. While you lay sleeping, no one can see you, but I watch you. My heart is full of love for you. What your heart is feeling right now as you watch your wife, what a parent feels watching a child, is a little picture for you, a gift, so you can know – every night when you go to sleep – that this is my heart for you. I want you to reflect on this at night before you close your eyes. I'm watching you, and I'm full of love." These were not just thoughts about God, but thoughts from God. I felt that God wanted to speak of his love to me – personally.[32]

All of this indicates how essential it is to pay attention to everyday fleeting ideas and feelings. They are the stuff of divine communication.

[32] Ortberg, John. *The Life You've Always Wanted: Spiritual Disciplines for Ordinary People* (Grand Rapids: Zondervan, 1997) p. 141.

Until fairly recently I have lived my entire life in parsonages. My dad was a Baptist pastor whose churches all provided a house. The churches I have served did the same. I thought I would live in a parsonage until I retired. Then one day as I was walking home, the question popped into my head, "Why don't you buy a house?" I had never entertained the idea before. My wife was resistant, but soon came around. I approached the Trustees and, miracle of miracles, they approved of the proposal and we quickly worked out a mutually acceptable housing allotment. Linda and I began the search and amazingly the perfect house with motivated sellers came on the market. We struck deal in a matter of days. The whole process

> *"Our failure to hear God has its deepest roots in a failure to understand, accept and grow into a conversational relationship with God, the sort of relationship suited to friends who are mature personalities in a shared enterprise."*
>
> *Dallas Willard*

took four months! Our home has been one of the great blessings of our lives. I am convinced that it was God who whispered, "Why don't you buy a house?"

In addition to ideas that come into our minds, God speaks by laying something on our hearts. For example, pastors often talk about experiencing "The Call" from God to enter full time Christian ministry. Something inside compels them to respond. Sometimes God speaks to us through things that excite or inspire us. Sometimes God speaks through things that trouble or upset us. The face of a starving child, the lifeless body of murdered teenager, a homeless person begging on the street might all be ways that God calls us to some great task.

These are some of the God's favored way of speaking.

116

The Silence of God

And yet many still claim that they have never heard God's voice. Why is that? Sometimes the reason we do not hear God is because he is not speaking. There are occasions when God remains silent. Such was the case in Israel about 3,000 years ago. "In those days the word of Lord was rare; there were not many visions." (I Samuel 3:1) Why was that? It was because of the wickedness of the people. God chose not to speak because he knew the people would not listen. Why should he waste his breath?

How sobering is that? If we have never heard God speak, it might because he has nothing to say to us.

If you find yourself in a position where you can honestly say, "God has never spoken to me," then you well might ask, "Why should God speak to me? What am I doing in life that would make speaking to me a reasonable thing for him to do? Are we in business together in life? Or am I in business just for myself, trying to 'use a little God' to advance my projects …Perhaps we do not hear the voice because we do not expect to hear it. Then again, perhaps we do not expect it because we know that we fully intend to run our lives on our own and have never seriously considered anything else.[33]

Dallas Willard insisted that hearing God is only possible for those who have developed an intimate relationship with the Lord. Those who hear have nurtured a friendship with Jesus by committing their lives to him and growing in discipleship through spiritual practices. He wrote,

In our attempts to understand how God speaks to us and guides us, we must above all hold on to the fact that this is to be sought only as a part of a certain

---

[33] Willard, op.cit. pp. 70, 71.

kind of life, a life of loving fellowship with the King and his other subjects within the kingdom of the heavens.[34]

But God's silence might have another explanation, one that is more positive. Perhaps God does not *need* to speak to us because we have reached a level of spiritual maturity that makes it unnecessary, at least when it comes to making decisions. For example, although I appreciate it when my children come to me for guidance, I do not want them to always be dependent on me. My responsibility as a parent includes instilling a set of values and guiding them into maturity so that they will know what is right without having to ask.

Willard writes,

There is something even greater than always knowing what is the right thing to do and always being directed by the present hand of God…The great height of our development as disciples of Christ is not that we should always be hearing God's voice but that we should have been trained under the hand of God – which includes hearing God as he speaks and guides - in such a way that we are able to stand at our appointed times and places in faith, hope and love even without a word from God.[35]

In the book of Hebrews the author writes, "In many and various ways God has spoken…" This chapter has touched on a few of the most common ways that God makes himself known. His preferred method is the "still, small voice." It is one that calls for attentive ears on our part. We can learn much from young Samuel who said, "Speak, Lord, for your servant listens."

For further reading:

Dallas Willard, "Hearing God

---

[34] Ibid. p. 31.
[35] Ibid., p. 209.

Discussion Guide

1. Ask the class, "Have you ever had an experience of God speaking to you? How did he speak? What was the message? How did you feel?" Give opportunities to share either with the whole group or in small circles.

2. Earlier in my ministry a clearly upset parishioner came to see me. He demanded, "Why doesn't God speak to me? I have asked him a hundred times, and still there is nothing but silence." How would you respond to such a question?

3. My friend's dilemma was because of his misunderstanding of the way that God speaks. He assumed that it was only in an audible voice. Is that the way many people think? What are some other ways people experienced God speaking to them?

4. Note that the primary way that God speaks his word to us is through the Bible. In the next chapter we will be exploring ways that we can experience a personal word from God in the pages of scripture.

5. In addition to scripture, Dallas Willard maintains that there are three primary ways that God speaks. They include:

- People
- Circumstances, especially coincidences and surprises
- Ideas in the mind and impressions on the heart

People

Dallas Willard wrote, "*No means of communication between God and us is more commonly used in the Bible or the history of the church than the voice of a definite, individual human being...I believe I can say with assurance that God's speaking in union with the human voice and human language is the primary objective way in which God addresses us."* ("Hearing God" p. 96, 97)

Ask the group to share an experience of a time when they sensed that God was speaking to them through the voice of another person.

Circumstances

In Frederick Meyer's book, "The Secret of Guidance," he wrote, *"The circumstances of our daily life are to us an infallible indication of God's will, when they concur with the inward promptings of the spirit and with the Word of God."* ("Hearing God" p. 170)

Ask the group to share a time when circumstances, especially coincidences and surprises, seem to have been the voice of God. Someone has observed, "For Christians there is no such thing as coincidences." Agree or disagree?

Ideas in the Mind and Impressions on the Heart

Willard wrote, *"The final means through which God addresses us is our own spirits – our own thoughts and feelings toward ourselves as well as toward events and people around us. This, I believe, is the primary subjective way in which God addresses us...For those who are living in harmony with God it most commonly comes in the form of their own thoughts and attendant feelings."* ("Hearing God" p .99, 100)

Ask the group to share a time when they sensed God speaking to them through ideas or impressions.

6. Is it possible to sense God speaking to us through people, circumstances and ideas/impressions and yet be mistaken? How do you respond to someone who says, "The Lord spoke to me and said..." Note that scripture calls on us to "test the spirits" with two

or more witnesses. These witnesses can be any of the items listed in the "Listening to God" handout.

7. Invite the group silently to think of one question or problem with which they are dealing. Have them pray using James Dobson's words, "Lord, I need to know what you want me to do, and I am listening. Please speak to me through my friends, books, magazines I pick up and read, and through circumstances." Willard wrote, "I am sure that it will work, if God has something, he really wants me to know or do. This is ultimately because I am sure of how great and good he is." ("Hearing God" pp. 199, 200)

Chapter Ten
Confession

Some time ago I participated in a wedding at a Roman Catholic Church. After the rehearsal I poked around the sanctuary when I came upon a confessional. Confessionals have long intrigued me, so mysterious and possessing a holy otherness that is foreign to my Baptist upbringing. I was curious see what the inside looked like, so I waited until nearly everyone was gone. When no one was looking I quietly opened the door and was shocked by what greeted me - brooms, a broken fan, old bulletins, a mop bucket, and dust – lots and lots of dust. This confessional had not been used for a long, long time.

> *"Ignatius had a strong conviction that without a deep sense of your own sinfulness and your absolute need for the salvation rendered in Christ, you will not truly be able to know and appreciate in a transformative way the cost God expanded on your behalf."*
>
> *Larry Warner*

This broom closet/confessional is symbolic. Confession has fallen out of favor, and not just within the Roman Catholic tradition. Protestants seldom, if ever, confess their sins. Even when we do, our confessions are generic. The best we can muster is the line in the Lord's Prayer when we ask, "Forgive us our debts, as we forgive our debtors." I wonder how God feels about this. "That's it? That's all you've got? After all the lousy things you have done?"

We need to confess our sins to God. This is not to be heard like a mother dragging her son by the ear and pointing to a broken cookie jar and demanding "fess up!" Neither is it to be taken as a prophetic warning of God's wrath. "Confess or you will burn in hell." The call for confession grows out of a concern that without it we will miss out on the greatest blessing a Christian can know. That is an *experience* of God's love, grace and forgiveness. Many of us have a theoretical understanding of this but have yet to personally receive it.

A few years ago a high school classmate died. At the wake, her husband, Curt, who was also a high school buddy, showed me some musical compositions she had written and recorded. They were all Christian numbers and included songs like, "Your Love" which contains the lines,

Your love comes over me
Like rivers of living water
Your love
It penetrates the stoniness of my hardened heart
Your love comes over me
Like rivers of living water
Refreshing me, thrilling me, cleansing my soul.
Your love, Your love.[36]

Curt said to me, "Harry, I don't get it. I know I am saved. I have been a Christian for forty years, but I never understood what she was talking about. I have never experienced that kind of love." I think he spoke for many of us.

One road that leads to an *experience* of God's love is paved by confession. Ignatius of Loyola wrote that without a deep sense of our own sinfulness we will never appreciate the depths of God's love, mercy, and forgiveness. This is why God encourages us to confess our sins. It is not that God needs it, but we do. Confession is not

---

[36] Words and Music by Dawn Carlson, copyright 1998.

designed to make us miserable, but to usher us into the fullness of life that comes through the touch of grace.

Psychologist and Spiritual Director David Brenner observed, "Every time I dare to meet God in the vulnerability of my sin and shame, this knowing (of love) is strengthened...I only know Divine, unconditional, radical and reckless love for me when I dare to approach God just as I am. The more I have the courage to meet God in this place of weakness, the more I will know myself to be truly and deeply loved by God."[37]

Ironically, the person who is in the best position to experience the enormity of God's love is the one who is the worst sinner. Only a prodigal knows the true depths of his father's love, a love that will forever escape an elder brother who keeps his nose clean. The good news (or bad, depending on how you look at it) is that we are all prodigals. We have all committed sins for which we need to confess. Therefore we all have the opportunity to experience God's love.

Unfortunately we are oblivious to most of our sinful behavior. As mentioned in chapter two, it is a spiritual truth that sin blinds us to our sinfulness.

> *An oracle is within my heart concerning the sinfulness of the wicked: There is no fear of God before his eyes. For in his own eyes he flatters himself too much to detect or hate his sin.* (Psalm 36: 1, 2)

Civil War historian James McPherson wrote about a plantation owner named James Hammond. A slave owner, he purchased an eighteen-year-old named Sally and her infant daughter Louisa. For years he made Sally his concubine, fathering several children, only to replace

---

[37] Benner, David G. *The Gift of Being Yourself: The Sacred Call to Self-Discovery* (Downers Grove, Illinois: InterVarsity Press, 2015) p. 49.

her with Louisa when she turned twelve. He also allegedly sexually abused four of his nieces. Later in life his wife left him, and an epidemic took the lives of many of his slaves and livestock. In his diary he wrote, "Great God, what have I done? Never was a man so cursed...what have I done or omitted to do to deserve this fate?" [38] Hammond was oblivious to his wickedness.

How much easier to see the speck in another's eye but ignore the log in our own! We need a spiritual shovel to unearth those sins that are buried in our subconscious. We need a pair of spiritual eyeglasses to compensate for our myopia.

In his book, "Prayer," Tim Keller wrote,

Confession should not be done simply as a response to a sin about which you are already aware and convicted. Our prayer life is the place where we should examine our lives and find the sins that otherwise we would be too insensitive or busy to acknowledge. We should have regular time of self-examination, using guidelines that come from biblical descriptions of what a Christian should be.[39]

Confession of sin is not limited to when we convert to Christ. It is one of our ongoing spiritual practices.

How do we go about this? What process will help us?

I. Pray That Our Eyes Be Opened

Because sin blinds us to our own sinfulness, we need the revealing work of the Holy Spirit to open our eyes so that we can recognize our transgressions. We get that help when we ask for it and then

---

[38] Ortberg, John. *The Life You've Always Wanted: Spiritual Disciplines for Ordinary People* (Grand Rapids: Zondervan) pp. 132, 133
[39] Keller, Timothy. *Prayer: Experiencing Awe and Intimacy with God* (New York: Dutton, 2014) p. 217.

open ourselves to receive it. We can cooperate with the Spirit by using the following tools.

II. Tools

The Story of the Fall

Read Genesis 3, the story of Adam and Eve's fall. This is not just a story about two people who lived a long time ago in a land far away. This is our story. We are Adam and Eve. Their sin is our sin, and it went deeper than stealing the forbidden fruit. This theft was more a symptom than the disease itself. The sin behind all sin is self-centeredness, the desire to be God and rule our own lives. That is what eating the fruit represented.

To what extent have we rejected God, or what is more common, put him on the sidelines of our lives? Is our life God-centered or self-centered? If the latter, we are drawn to sinful behavior like a magnet, whether it be lying, stealing or some other transgression.

The Ten Commandments

Martin Luther advocated using the Ten Commandments as a guide. We are to walk through these commandments and ask ourselves, "When have I violated this law in letter or in spirit?"

1. You shall have no other gods before me.
2. You shall not make for yourself an idol
3. You shall not misuse the name of the Lord your God
4. Remember the Sabbath day by keeping it holy.
5. Honor your father and your mother.
6. You shall not murder
7. You shall not commit adultery
8. You shall not steal

9. You shall not give false testimony

10. You shall not covet

The Seven Deadly Sins

Another useful instrument is the Seven Deadly Sins. Interestingly, all of these are sins of the spirit. They are attitudes and thoughts, rather than overt acts. They are called deadly because they inevitably lead to transgressions. Ask yourself, "Where in my life is there...?"

1. Pride
2. Envy
3. Anger
4. Lust
5. Gluttony
6. Sloth
7. Greed

Galatians 5

In Galatians 5:19-21 Paul outlines "The acts of the sinful nature." Review the list and ask yourself which of these are exercising control over your life.

1. Sexual immorality and impurity
2. Debauchery and orgies
3. Idolatry and witchcraft
4. Hatred, discord, fits of rage
5. Jealousy and envy
6. Selfish ambition
7. Dissensions and factions
8. Drunkenness

Such self-examination could lead to despair. No doubt it will unless we are first convinced of God's love for us. There is a difference between conviction of sin, sometimes called "godly sorrow," and condemnation As discussed in chapter two, conviction is feeling bad or guilty about something we have *done*. Condemnation is feeling bad about who we *are*. If we feel condemned, we can be sure it is not of God. Sinking into these feelings is a sign that we need to back off and spend time bathing in God's love. Ignatius of Loyola would not permit his sensitive friend, Peter Favre (co-founder of the Jesuit order), to examine his sinfulness for four years. Such was his need to first be grounded in God's love. Recall these words, "How great is the love the Father has lavished on us, that we should be called children of God! And that is what we are!" (I John 3:1) Only when we are convinced of this are we in a position to examine ourselves.

III. Confess Our Failures

We next reflect on how we would feel if the world knew of our sin. Imagine the shame and embarrassment. What is the just punishment for such crimes? We confess our sorrow for our transgressions, asking for God's forgiveness and mercy. Those of the Roman Catholic tradition will want to seek out a priest. Others might prefer to confess to God in the privacy of their hearts,

IV. Hear God's Word of Pardon

Next, remember that Jesus paid for our sins. He stepped forward and said, "I will take your shame, your embarrassment and your punishment. Give them to me."

Reflect on these words of grace. As we meditate on these truths, we will be overwhelmed by the depths of God's love for us.

He was wounded for our transgressions, he was bruised for our iniquities; upon him was the chastisement that made us whole, and with his stripes we are healed. (Isaiah 53: 5)

If we confess our sins, he is faithful and just and will forgive us our sins and purify us from all unrighteousness. (I John 1.9)

I, I am the Lord, and beside me there is no savior. I, I am He who blots out your transgressions for my sake, and I will not remember your sins. (Isaiah 43:11, 25)

There is now no condemnation for those who are in Christ Jesus. (Romans 8:1)

On Sunday mornings we are encouraged to bring our very best and present it to the Lord. We offer God our best efforts, offerings, and praise. We are also called to bring our worst to God. In Psalm 51 David wrote, "You do not delight in sacrifice, or I would bring it; you do not take pleasure in burnt offerings. The sacrifices of God are a broken spirit, a broken and contrite heart, O God, you will not despise."

William Sangster was a gifted Methodist preacher in the United Kingdom. His sermons were not only insightful, but passionate and grace filled. Sangster was a humble soul who radiated Christ. What was the secret to his effectiveness? After his death, his son found an inventory of his life, taking the form of a confession. Sangster wrote:

I am a minister of God and yet my private life is a failure in these ways:

- *I am irritable and easily put out*

- *I am impatient with my wife and children*

- *I am deceitful in that I often express private annoyance when a caller is announced and simulate pleasure when I actually greet them*

• *Most of my study has been crudely ambitious*

• *Even in my preaching I fear that I am more often wondering what people think about me, than what they think about my Lord and His word*

• *I find slight envies in my heart at the greater success of other young ministers. I seem to match myself with them and am vaguely jealous when they attract more notice than I do*

Much of the power of his pulpit ministry was derived from his honesty before God. As a result of his confession, he knew in a deep and personal way the grace and forgiveness of his Lord as well as the renewing power to live a better life.

We need to confess. Confession will usher us into an experience of God's love and grace.

For further reading:

Tim Keller, "Prayer" (Chapter 13)

Tim Muldoon, "The Ignatian Workout" (Chapter 5)

John Ortberg, "The Life You've Always Wanted) (Chapter 8)

Larry Warner, "Journey with Jesus" (Part 3, Week 1)

Discussion Guide

(Note: Some of these exercises are similar to those in Chapter Two)

1. Let's play a word association game. I will say a word and you will write down one, two or three words that jump into your mind.

• Lemon

- Paper
- Fall
- Animal
- Sin

2. Imagine that before class a spaceship lands right in front of you and out toddles ET. He asks you what you are doing, and you respond, "I am going to that church for a class on sin." ET gets a puzzled look on his face as he leafs through his English/Martian dictionary. "I do not seem to find this word in my book. Can you define 'sin' for me?" What would you say?

3. Read Genesis 3. What was Adam and Eve's sin(s)? What did eating the forbidden fruit represent? What were the consequences of their actions? *Point out that sin is a state of being, rather than a specific act. The sin that is behind all sins is self-centeredness, i.e., the desire to be like God. This inevitably leads to individual transgressions. These sins are symptoms of the more serious disease.*

4. "It is a spiritual reality that sins blind us to our own sinfulness." Agree or disagree? Why? Where do you see examples of this?

5. One way to open our eyes to unrecognized sins is to use the tools that were introduced in the chapter. Distribute copies of the Ten Commandments. Invite the class members to break up and retire to a quiet corner. Which of these laws have they violated either in letter or spirit? How would they feel if their classmates knew their secret? Give ten or fifteen minutes.

6. Regroup and read the Parable of the Prodigal Son. (Luke 15:11-24) What was the Prodigal's sin(s)? What did he deserve? What do you think he felt as he made his way back home? How did his father receive him? How do you think he felt?

7. Imagine you are on the road to meet your Father in Heaven. In light of your sins, how do you feel? In your mind's eye, see him run out to you, embrace you, kiss you and clothe you in a fine robe and shoes. How do you feel?

8. Does this exercise help you to experience God's love?

9. Read Psalm 32:1-5 as a closing prayer.

> *Blessed is he whose transgression is forgiven; whose sins are covered.*
> *Blessed is the man whose sin the Lord does not count against him*
> *and in whose spirit, there is no deceit.*
> *When I kept silent, my bones wasted away*
> *through my groaning all day long.*
> *For day and night your hand was heavy upon me;*
> *My strength was sapped as in the heat of summer.*
> *Then I acknowledged my sin to you, and I did not cover up my iniquity.*
> *I said, "I will confess my transgressions to the Lord"-*
> *And you forgave the guilt of my sin.*

Chapter Eleven

Scripture

The story is told of two men arguing about who knew the Bible the best. One of them challenged the other saying, "You think you are so smart. I'll bet you don't even know the Lord's Prayer. I'll give you twenty dollars if you can recite it." The other man countered, "I'll take that bet." Closing his eyes and folding his hands, he began, "Now I lay me down to sleep, I pray the Lord my soul to keep…" The other man stared at him in disbelief and said, "By golly, you do know the Lord's Prayer. Here is your twenty dollars."

For many, the Bible is a dusty, dry book. It is big and intimidating. Much of it is hard to understand. No wonder we avoid reading it. As a consequence biblical illiteracy is rampant within the Christian community.

This chapter introduces the spiritual discipline of reading the scriptures. The Bible is the clearest and most reliable way that God speaks. That is why it is called "God's Word." And God does not speak in some general, generic way. Dietrich Bonhoeffer explained,

In our meditation we ponder the chosen text on the strength of the promise that it has something utterly personal to say to us for this day and for our Christian life, that it is not only God's Word for the Church, but also God's Word for us individually.[40]

---

[40] Bonhoeffer, Dietrich *Life Together* (New York: HarperCollins, 1954) p. 82.

This is why reading scripture is an essential part of our daily practice. John Ortberg wrote, "I have never known someone leading a spiritually transformed life who had not been deeply saturated in Scripture." [41]

Since God uses scripture to speak a personal message to us, reading the Bible should be a rich experience. When the prophet Ezekiel was commanded to eat the scroll, he found that it tasted as sweet as honey. The Psalmist, Jeremiah and the Apostle John all reported the same.

And yet so many of us neither know nor love the Bible. How can it come alive for us? How can it become as sweet as honey? There are at least three ways.

> *"In this business of living the Christian life, ranking high among the most neglected aspects is one having to do with the reading of the Christian scriptures. Not that Christians don't or won't read their Bibles. And not that Christians don't believe that their Bibles are the word of God. What is neglected is reading the Scriptures formatively, reading in order to live."*
>
> *Eugene Peterson*

- Suffering and Trouble
- Imaginative Meditation
- Lectio Divina

Suffering and Trouble

No one seeks out suffering and trouble. And yet these clouds have silver linings. It is amazing how the scriptures come alive as we find ourselves in distress. When John Bunyan was arrested and thrown

---

[41] Ortberg, John. *The Life You've Always Wanted* (Grand Rapids: Zondervan, 1997) p. 181.

into prison for six years, he wrote, "I never had in all my life so great an insight into the word of God as now. The scriptures that I saw nothing in before were made in this place and condition to shine upon me. Jesus Christ also was never more real and apparent than now." [42]

This has been the experience of many. In times of heartache we instinctively turn to the Bible, only to discover that overnight it has become a whole new book! The texts that we might have read dozens of times before now speak with surprising power. Books that had been dull are now aflame with life, offering comfort, reassurance, and hope. We resonate with Tevye in "Fiddler on the Roof" who sang, "If I were a rich man...I'd discuss the holy books with the learned men, several hours every day. That would be the sweetest thing of all."

But where exactly do we turn for help in times of crisis? We cannot just open it up anyplace and hope that a solution will magically appear.

The Gideons' web site offers "Bible Verses for Your Special Needs." It identifies helpful texts for various times of trouble. These verses function like a life saver thrown to a drowning man. We cling to them to keep our noses above the tumult until our rescue comes.

The Bible comes alive in times of suffering and trouble.

Imaginative Meditation

The second way to make the Bible come alive is by using our imaginations. This is not some new fad. It is a practice that has been used for more than five hundred years. Ignatius called it "Imaginative

---

[42] Bunyon, John. *Grace Abounding to the Chief of Sinners* (Evangelical Press, 1978) p. 123.

Prayer." By using our imaginations we do more than read the Bible, we actually enter into it. We try to put ourselves in the story and experience the event. It is an especially useful technique for reading the Gospel stories of Jesus. If we want to know Jesus in a more personal way, there is no better way than through Imaginative Prayer.

What are the steps?

First, we choose a story to which we feel drawn. This is the Holy Spirit's way of directing us. But it is not necessary to feel pulled to any particular story. They can all speak in powerful ways. Some of the most profound experiences I have had occurred when I wrestled with texts that at first seemed to offer nothing.

Second, read the story through three or four times. All we are doing at this stage is familiarizing ourselves with the text. For the purpose of this exercise, let us use the story of Jesus stilling the storm as recorded in Mark 4:35-41.

That day when evening came, he said to his disciples, "Let us go over to the other side." Leaving the crowd behind, they took him along, just as he was, in the boat. There were also other boats with him. A furious squall came up, and the waves broke over the boat, so that it was nearly swamped. Jesus was in the stern, sleeping on a cushion. The disciples woke him and said to him, "Teacher, don't you care if we drown?"

He got up, rebuked the wind and said to the waves, "Quiet! Be still!" Then the wind died down and it was completely calm.

He said to his disciples, "Why are you so afraid? Do you still have no faith?"

They were terrified and asked each other, "Who is this? Even the wind and waves obey him!"

The third step is where we put our imaginations to work. Use all five senses to flesh out the story. Walk through the story five times, concentrating on one sense each trip.

- *See* – Visualize the pounding waves, the lightning flashes, the rocking boat, Jesus asleep in the stern.

- *Hear* – Listen to the howling wind, the flapping sails, the thunderclaps, the creaking boat, and the crying voices.

- *Feel* – Feel the cold spray, drenched clothing, the tossing boat, fatigue and fear.

- *Smell* – Sniff the sea air, the fishy odor, the smell of wet wool.

- *Taste* – Taste the sweat mixed with the sea water.

The fourth step is to make connections with the story. This narrative is not just the story of people who lived long ago in a place far away. This is also our story. We are in there someplace. We recall stormy times when we felt swamped and doomed. We remember situations when we have been frightened and Jesus seemed fast asleep. Alternatively, make connections with the characters in the story. With whom do we identify? Depending on the story, it might be the disciples, the Pharisees, the crowd or Jesus himself.

The fifth step is to listen to Jesus. This is the payoff for all our hard work. What is Jesus saying in this story? What is his personal word for us? Have an imaginary conversation with him.

Jesuit Priest James Martin shares the story of how God spoke to him through this story and exercise.

The next day, I returned to the scene in my imagination. As soon as I climbed into the boat, a word popped into my head: swamped. The boat was taking on water during the violent storm, being swamped and the disciples were terrified. Swamped was the word I used frequently with friends to describe my daily life. I was forever racing among a variety of projects and often felt overwhelmed...I (then) imagined myself standing on the sunny shore of the Sea of Galilee, after the storm passed. Then I imagined telling Jesus how swamped I felt. Sitting on the beach and airing out my feelings felt freeing. What a relief to share this with Jesus...In prayer, I asked Jesus how he was able to juggle everything, how he was able to handle all the demands on his time. An answer suggested itself: Jesus took things as they came and trusted that God was bringing things before him, rather than trying to plan everything. He also accepted the need to withdraw from the crowds sometimes... (I realized that) Jesus would be in the boat with me. I had nothing to fear. That insight gave me enormous peace. No longer did I feel swamped, because I realized that I had a choice in life."[43]

Through Imaginative Prayer we experience Christ speaking to us his personal word.

Lectio Divina

The third method of making the Bible come alive is called Lectio Divina, which means "Divine Reading." This is an ancient practice, dating back to the Desert Fathers of the third and fourth centuries. It is especially useful for non-narrative books such as the Psalms, Prophets and Epistles.

Lectio is a slow way of reading the Bible. I recently heard of a Benedictine monk who was working his way through the Psalms. He had spent eighteen months in the endeavor and was only up to Psalm

---

[43] Marin, James. *The Jesuit Guide to Almost Everything: A Spirituality for Real Life* (New York: HarperCollins, 2010) pp. 153, 154.

22! His is an extreme example, but it reminds us that in Lectio we do not rush through the scripture. We take our time.

There are four steps.

- Reading
- Reflecting
- Responding
- Resting

Let's use these steps to reflect on Isaiah 43:1-3

> *But now, this is what the Lord says –*
> *He who created you, O Jacob,*
> *He who formed you, O Israel:*
> *"Fear not, for I have redeemed you;*
> *I have summoned you by name; you are mine.*
> *When you pass through the waters,*
> *I will be with you;*
> *And when you pass through the rivers,*
> *they will not sweep over you.*
> *When you walk through the fire,*
> *you will not be burned;*
> *the flames will not set you ablaze.*
> *For I am the Lord, your God,*
> *the Holy One of Israel, your Savior."*

1. *Reading* – Slowly read through the text several times. Pay attention to when a word or a phrase begins to stand out. It is generally a subtle "shimmering." This is the way that the Holy Spirit whispers, "Pay attention. There is something important here." At this point, all we are looking for is the word or phrase that emerges. We are not seeking a message, but only to "catch the scent" of something special.

2. *Reflecting* – The second step is to meditate on this word or phrase. Sit quietly and contemplate it. An image that might be helpful is a cow chewing its cud. Perhaps a more appealing image is that of sucking on a piece of hard candy. Popular preacher Gardner Taylor advises "brooding" over the text. As we repeat the phrase over and over, notice what happens. For example, a few days ago I was using Lectio as I read Psalm 149. The phrase "The Lord delights in his people" stood out. As I meditated on it, the phrase changed to "The Lord delights in me." I knew that God loved and forgave me, but it never occurred to me that he might delight in me. My thoughts then turned to what delights me most. That was easy. It is my three grandchildren. I adore them. With a start I realized that God delights in me in the same way! What is God saying in a word or phrase from Isaiah 43?

3. *Responding* – The third step is responding to what our reflection has revealed. It might be a prayer of thanksgiving and praise. It could also be a confession of sin and plea for forgiveness. Maybe it is a decision to repent or change. Some people tap into their creative spirits and write a poem, sing a song or paint a picture.

4. *Resting* – The final step is to rest with Jesus. Simply spend time in God's presence. It is like sitting in a porch swing with a loved one on a summer evening. No one speaks, but both are silently enjoying each another's company. This is the goal of Lectio Divina. It is not meant to lead to deeper understanding of some Bible text, but to bring one into a personal encounter with God.

In summary, the Bible is the primary way that God speaks to us. Although it is sometimes a hard book to understand, the suggestions in this chapter will help it come alive.

There is something else that is fundamental to bringing the scriptures to life. That is the spirit with which we approach the text. When

Augustine was an inquisitive youth of eighteen, he tried reading the Bible in his quest for truth. But he came at it with a cynical, critical eye. He was appalled by its inelegant language and crude stories. Not surprisingly, he got nothing out of it. Neither will we if we approach it with the same spirit.

When Augustine became a Christian at the age of thirty-two, he returned to read it again. Now it spoke to him as never before. It had become a delight. He said, "Some people say, 'I have to see to believe.' But I have discovered 'I have to believe to see.'" If we believe the Bible offers God's personal word, we will see it too.

God's Word is often referred to as the *Holy* Bible. One of the marks of its holiness is the way God uses it to speak a personal word to every reader, no matter what level of maturity or intelligence. As someone observed, "The Bible is shallow enough for a child to wade in and deep enough for an elephant to swim."

For further reading:

Pennington, M. Basil "Lectio Divina: Renewing the Ancient Practice of Praying the Scriptures"

Peterson, Eugene "Eat This Book"

Discussion Guide

1. Rate your experience of reading the Bible from one to ten. One is "Dry as Dust" and ten is "Alive with Power." Explain your answer.

2. What is your favorite verse, passage or Bible story? What makes it so special?

3. Scripture comes alive to us through:

- Suffering
- Imaginative Prayer
- Lectio Divina

4. Suffering

Read the following quote from a New Testament scholar. *"One of God's gifts to us in suffering is that we are granted to see and experience depths of his Word that a life of ease would never yield. Martin Luther had discovered the same 'Method' of seeing God in his Word. He said there are three rules for understanding Scripture: praying, meditating and suffering trials. The 'trials,' he said, are supremely valuable: they 'teach you not only how to know and understand but also to experience how right, how true, how sweet, how lovely, how mighty, how comforting God's word is: it is wisdom supreme.' Therefore the devil himself becomes the unwitting teacher of God's word."*

What do you think of this quote? Can you share a time when this was true for you?

5. Imaginative Prayer

Use the exercise offered in chapter six. Prepare copies of Mark 4:35-41.

- Read through the story two or three times to familiarize yourself with it.

- Read through it five more times, each time focusing on one of the five senses.

- What connections do you make with the story?

- Have a conversation with Jesus. What did you say? How did he respond?

6. Lectio Divina

Prepare copies of Isaiah 43:1-3.

- *Read* through the text three to five times, paying attention to any word or phrase that seems to "shimmer"

- *Reflect* on that word or phrase, saying it to yourself over and over. What happened?

- *Respond* to what you have experienced. Does it lead you to thanks, trust, repentance or what?

- *Rest* quietly in God's presence and goodness.

Note: There will probably not be sufficient time or energy to do both the Imaginative Prayer and Lectio Divina. Choose the one that you believe will be most helpful.

Chapter Twelve
Spirituality in Everyday Life

A few years ago one of our church vans needed some body work. A driver had cut the corner of the building a little too close and left a gash in the side. We took the vehicle to a nearby collision shop. The owner was known to be a Christian. He was active in his church, providing both leadership and financial support. In the waiting room were religious pictures and tracts. I later learned, however, that he talked the talk better than he walked the walk. He had a reputation for berating his staff and being slow to pay his vendors. Those who worked for him grumbled about some of his questionable business practices.

Evidently this shop-owner had compartmentalized his faith. His Christianity was confined to his morning devotions and Sunday worship. It failed to extend into his daily life.

Spirituality is not limited to one slice of the day. It is meant to infuse the entirety of it. Discipleship is a whole way of life. Every moment of every day provides the opportunity to live as a follower of Jesus. St. Benedict envisioned Christian spirituality as baptizing every aspect of life. It impacts how we eat, dress, work, use our time, treat other people, study, and spend money – everything.

"In Jesus' Name"

No doubt Benedict was influenced by what Paul wrote in Colossians 3:17. "And whatever you do, whether in word or deed, *do it all in the name of Jesus.*" We are to do everything in Jesus' name. But what does that mean? What does doing all in the name of Christ look like?

To do something in the name of someone means to conduct ourselves as he would if he were in our place. To do something in Jesus' name is to perform it in a way that is consistent with his character.[44] That means doing every day, ordinary tasks with a spirit of love. Spirituality writer Esther de Waal wrote,

Seeking God does not demand the unusual, the spectacular, the heroic. It asks of me as wife, mother, and housewife that I do the most ordinary, often dreary and humdrum things that face me each day, with a loving openness that will allow them to become my own immediate way to God.[45]

What would a life lived in Jesus' name look like?

What would it mean to *wake up* in Jesus' name? Some of us have a hard time getting out of bed. We are ugly in both mood and appearance. A woman was asked, "Do you wake up grumpy in the morning?" To which she replied, "No, I usually just let him sleep." To wake up in Jesus' name would be to open our eyes with a prayer of thanks for another day of life and a request for God's blessings upon it.

"The spirituality that emerges from the Rule of Benedict is a spirituality charged with living the ordinary life extraordinarily well. Here transforming life rather than transcending it is what counts. That is why the Rule of Benedict is meant for hard-working, busy people whose family lives and bills and civic duties and hard work consume them in this world today as well as for those who have dedicated themselves to living a publicly professed religious life."

Joan Chittister

---

[44] Title and general content of this section is credited to Ortberg, John. *The Life You've Always Wanted: Spiritual Disciplines for Ordinary People* (Grand Rapids: Zondervan, 1997) *Chapter 12.*

[45] DeWaal, Esther. *Seeking God: The Way of St. Benedict* (Collegeville, Minnesota: The Liturgical Press, 2001) pp. 7, 8.

What would it mean to *eat our meals* in Jesus' name? For many families, mealtime is rushed through in silence, accompanied by an occasional grunt. Some seldom even sit down at the table together. If Jesus sat at our meals it would be different. He would ask about our day, tell a joke, share a story, listen and offer encouragement. What a difference that could make. National Public Radio broadcast an interview with the author of "Confessions of a Boy-Crazy Girl." She related that although her father loved her, he had a hard time expressing it. He never told her that she was pretty or special. She could not recall a time when he expressed affection by word or touch. She hungered for this, and when she became an adolescent she sought it in other places. Not surprisingly her search led to a series of unhealthy relationships. How much different her life might have been if her dad had eaten meals with her in Jesus' name.

What would it mean to *drive* in Jesus' name? We would toot the horn less frequently and step on the accelerator more gently. We would allow other cars to merge and would keep to the speed limit. We would listen to something different on the radio or turn it off entirely, using the time to commune with God.

What would it mean to *converse* in Jesus' name? It would involve less talking and more listening. Someone who practiced such Christlikeness was Joseph Cardinal Bernardin.

When I took part in parish receptions, I tried to look everyone in the eye and make each person feel that he or she was important, the only one present at the moment...Somehow, when you make that eye contact, when you convince people that you really care and that, even if hundreds of others are around, at that particular moment they are the only ones that count – then you establish a new relationship. They leave feeling that they have entered into a special intimacy with you – if only for a moment. They sense that somehow you truly care about them and that, more importantly, you have somehow mediated the love, mercy, and compassion of the Lord.[46]

We could go down the list. What would it mean to choose our entertainment, spend our money and discipline our children in Jesus' name?

Trappist Monk Thomas Merton described such a life as, "…doing ordinary things quietly and perfectly for the glory of God."[47]

We are created to make a difference in this world. Psalm 84 paints a lovely image. The Psalmist observed pilgrims on their way to Jerusalem. He wrote, "As they pass through the Valley of Baca, they make it a place of springs." That is the kind of impact we are meant to make. As we pass through dry and dusty places, we transform them into verdant valleys.

Work: A Gift from God to Us

We spend the bulk of our daily lives at work. The manner in which we perform our job is a form of spirituality.

In ancient Rome manual labor was regarded with disdain. Work was for slaves, servants or the poor. The good life was one of leisure. No doubt many early Christians shared this view.

But in the 5th century St. Benedict offered a different perspective. When he founded the monastic movement that is called by his name, he incorporated six hours of physical labor into the daily schedule of every monk. No one was excluded. The Abbot had to wash pots and pans and sweep the floor just like everyone else. Even the sick and infirm were given jobs that they could do in their beds. Benedict

---

[46] Bernardin, Joseph Louis. *The Gift of Peace: Personal Reflections by Joseph Cardinal Bernardin* (Chicago: Loyola Press, 1997) P. 82.
[47] DeWaal, op. cit., p. 30.

insisted on this because he saw work as a privilege, not a punishment; a gift, not a curse. It was a sacred duty not to be denied to anyone. He taught that "Idleness is the enemy of the soul." (Rule of Benedict 48.24)

What were the blessings that Benedict recognized?

1. Work gives meaning and purpose to life

Every believer has a vocation from God. Each of us has a calling from God. We were created to be and do something. God has equipped us with special spiritual gifts that will enable us to fulfill that calling. In addition, he instills a passion for some cause or work. There are some things that will not be accomplished unless we fulfill that vocation.

The discovery of that calling is one of the keys to a rich and happy life. Fulfilling our life's work brings wholeness. More than that, it provides the resource to endure unimaginable suffering. Viktor Frankl was a psychotherapist who survived the Nazi concentration camps. There he discovered how crucial a sense of meaning was for survival. In "Man's Search for Meaning" he wrote,

According to logotherapy, the striving to find a meaning in one's life is the primary motivational force in man…A man who becomes conscious of the responsibility he bears toward a human being who affectionately waits for him, or to an unfinished work, will never be able to throw away his life. He knows the "why" for his existence and will be able to bear almost any "how."[48]

It is a blessing to know that our lives have meaning and that we are created to make a difference.

---

[48] Frankl, Viktor. *Man's Search for Meaning: An Introduction to Logotherapy* (New York: Washington Square, 1963) pp. 154, 127.

2. Work brings us closer to God

Benedict taught that as we work, we are co-creators and co-laborers with God. Although God rested on the seventh day, when the Sabbath was over, he went back to the timeclock and punched in. Scripture teaches that God continues to work to redeem this world When we work, we are partnering with God in this great venture. Like Adam, we are joining with God to care for his creation.

In Benedictine spirituality, work is what we do to continue what God wanted done. Work is co-creative. Keeping a home that is beautiful and ordered and nourishing and artistic is co-creative. Working in a machine shop that makes gears for tractors is co-creative… In Benedictine spirituality, work is purposeful and perfecting and valuable. It is not a time-filler or a money-maker or a necessary evil. We work because the world is unfinished, and it is ours to develop.[49]

Our calling is to be stewards of God's creation. Since God made everything, everything that exists is sacred and belongs to him. This brings dignity and sacredness to whatever we are doing. We feel a connection to God as we work. This is especially true when we are gardening, building, cleaning or repairing.

3. Work brings us closer to one another

Benedict taught that work builds connection and community. Oftentimes what makes work such drudgery is that all we can see is what is right in front of us. We feel like a cog in a machine. Those who work on an assembly line in my hometown of Flint, Michigan complain of this. Many see their work as tightening the same bolt over and over again and even refer to themselves as "shop rats." Benedict sought to alter this perspective.

---

[49] Chittister, Joan. *Wisdom Distilled from the Daily: Living the Rule of St. Benedict Today* (New York: HarperCollins, 1990) p. 86.

First, Benedict instructs us to see our work as a crucial component in a long process. We are connected with people who come before and after us. For example, the baker must see himself as part of a process that began months ago when someone else tilled the soil and planted the seed. He is also connected to the person who harvested the grain and milled the wheat. He is followed by people who will slice and serve the bread as well as those who will clean up. No person is more important than another. All are essential and connected.

Secondly, Benedict reminds us that our jobs are part of a grand venture. He wants us to keep in mind the ultimate results of our labor. The baker is not just baking bread but feeding the community. The factory worker is not just tightening bolts but building a safe and comfortable vehicle for a family to enjoy for years to come. An investment banker is not just making money but providing retirement income for senior citizens on limited incomes.

Work is God's gift to us.

Work: A Gift from Us to God

Work is also our gift to God, provided we go about it in the right way. That way, of course, is doing it "in Jesus' name." This means to do it in his character, as he would if he were in our place. What would this look like? Once again, St. Benedict offered helpful suggestions.

1. At the start of each workday, pray to be a blessing to others.

Dietrich Bonhoeffer said that, "The prayers of the morning determine the day. Wasted time, which we are ashamed of, temptations that beset us, weakness and listlessness in our work, disorder and indiscipline in our thinking and our relations with other people very frequently have their cause in neglect of the morning prayer."[50] What a difference it makes when we begin our labors with a prayer that our work might be a blessing to others. This is true no matter what the job. Benedict taught that no kind of work is more important than another. The work of the ditch digger is just as holy as that of the priest leading worship. All labor is sacred, if presented as an offering to God.

Some years ago I attended the worship service at the Maranatha Baptist Church in Plains, Georgia where former President Jimmy Carter is a member. It is a small congregation unable to afford a custodian's services. Every member was expected to pitch in to help. The bulletin listed the assignments for the upcoming week. Jimmy Carter was given the task of mowing the lawn and trimming the bushes. His wife, Rosalyn Carter, was scheduled to clean the nursery. Benedict would have smiled at that!

2. Pause and pray before each task, asking for efficiency, diligence and effectiveness

Pastor Erwin Lutzer of Moody Church in Chicago confessed that every day as he enters his office, he is overwhelmed by the work that greets him. Scores of e-mails and letters await a response. Phone messages demand his attention. He needs to study for Sunday's sermon, write articles and attend meetings. How does he handle the pressure? Every morning he prays, "By faith I believe you are with me, Lord. And by faith I believe you will help me accomplish the work you have set before me." God has never let him down!

---

[50] Bonhoeffer, Dietrich. *Life Together: The Classic Exploration of Christian Community* (New York: HarperCollins, 1954) p. 71.

3. *Work at a steady, even, stately pace*

We are to go about our tasks with diligence and focus, avoiding desperation and frenzy. We concentrate and pace ourselves, remembering that life is a marathon, not a hundred-yard dash.

Neither should we work in a lazy, haphazard manner. Avoid daydreaming and sloppiness, being good stewards of our time and talents.

4. *"Do what you are doing"*

Benedict would have frowned on multi-tasking. His counsel was to concentrate on one job at a time. We are to avoid distractions, focusing on what lies in front of us. We are to strive to be present in the moment.

(My wife, who works at a high-pressure job in the Chicago Loop, took exception with this advice. She complained that without multi-tasking she could never get her work done! Duly noted. I promised her I would register her counterpoint. Regrettably, there are those who do not have the luxury to "do what you are doing." But it is something for which to strive.)

5. *Treat all tools with reverence*

Benedict is famous for saying, "The plow and hoe of the shed are as sacred as the chalice of the altar." They are all to be treated with the same respect and care, since they are all created by God and belong to him. Everyone has tools, whether they are shovels, pens or computers. Everyone has a space to tend. Treat them with reverence.

6. *No grumbling or murmuring*

In II Corinthians 9 the Apostle Paul writes that "God loves a cheerful giver." The corollary is "God loves a cheerful worker." If we grumble and complain when we give our offerings or when we perform our jobs, they lose their acceptability to God. As one of my seminary professors once said, "It is not enough to *do and say* Christian things. We also need to do and say them in a *Christ-like way.*" Resentment is never Christ-like.

7. *Do ordinary things extraordinarily well*

As mentioned earlier, Thomas Merton advised, "Do your work quickly and perfectly for the glory of God." On occasion we are all tempted to "phone it in." But the sacredness of work is lost in the process. Doing ordinary things extraordinarily well restores that holiness. The story is told of a sculptor who was diligently working on the backside of a statue which was to be placed in St. Peter's Cathedral. An observer remarked, "Why are you spending so much time on that? You know it is going to be in a corner. No one will see the back." To which the sculptor replied, "God will." May we all have that kind of devotion!

Even mundane work can be performed with holy diligence. A friend of mine commented on a local Burger King that was always immaculate. The place was spotless. He and his wife were curious about this. One day they observed an older employee faithfully cleaning up after every customer. She was meticulous about the dining room under her care. She was doing an ordinary thing extraordinarily well.

8. Avoid letting work define us, either positively or negatively

One of the first questions we ask when meeting someone new is, "What kind of work do you do?" Much of our identity and sense of worth is tied up with our jobs. This is not healthy. It is not helpful for someone with a so-called menial job. They can feel worthlessness and a failure. But neither is it good for a person in a high prestige position. They are susceptible to pride, arrogance and insensitivity.

Our worth is not determined by the work we do, but who we are in Christ. Our primary identity is as God's beloved child. Never forget that!

9. Present our labor as an offering, serving others as if they were Christ

This sums up everything above. Our work is a kind of prayer that we offer to God. We glorify or besmirch his name by the way we go about our tasks.

In the Rule of Benedict he says, "Hour by hour keep careful watch over all you do, aware that God's gaze is upon you, wherever you may be." (RB 4.49) And in Jesus' Parable of the Talents he indicates that there is a day of accounting awaiting us. We will have to report how we used our time and our talents. On that day what will matter is not only the work we have done, but the manner in which we have performed it. May we all testify that we performed our work "in Jesus' name." And may we all hear the words, "Well done, good and faithful servant."

For further reading:

Dietrich Bonhoeffer, "Life Together"

Joan Chittister, "Wisdom Distilled from the Daily: Living the Rule of St. Benedict"

Esther de Waal, "Seeking God: The Way of St. Benedict"

Jane Tomaine, "St. Benedict's Toolbox: The Nuts and Bolts of Everyday Benedictine

Discussion Guide

1. What are your regular spiritual practices and how much time do you spend observing them?

2. Have each person write down a list of all the things they do during the day, starting from the time they wake up. Read Colossians 3:17. "Whatever you do, in word or deed, do everything in the name of the Lord Jesus, giving thanks to God the Father through him." Explain that to do something "in the name of Jesus" is to do it as he would if he were in our place. Have the group silently and slowly read through their list, thinking about what it would look like to do these things "in Jesus' name." Invite them to share their discoveries.

3. Ask the group to rate their work from one to ten on how meaningful and/or enjoyable it is. One means miserable, dull and purposeless. Ten means enriching, enjoyable and rewarding. Why did they give these scores?

4. Work: God's Gift to Us

Explain that Benedict viewed work not as a curse, but a blessing. He offered ways in which we can infuse our labor with sacredness, finding meaning in whatever we do. Introduce and briefly explain the following.

- Work gives meaning and purpose to life (Note: Finding your vocation will be discussed in detail in chapter 17)

- Work brings us closer to God

- Work brings us closer to one another

Ask if any have had these experiences. Invite them to reflect on how their work might be different if they took these truths to heart.

5. Work: Our Gift to God

God is not only praised through worship, music and prayer. He is also glorified by the way we go about our daily tasks. Introduce and briefly explain each of these Benedictine principles.

- Pray each morning to be a blessing to someone

- Pray before each task, asking for diligence and efficiency

- Work at a steady, even pace

- Do what you are doing

- Treat all tools with respect

- No grumbling or complaining

- Do ordinary things extraordinarily well

- Do not let your work define you

- Present your work as an offering to God

Which of these do they think they could incorporate into their work? What difference would it make?

Chapter Thirteen
Church Life

So far, we have looked at spiritual disciplines that can be practiced in solitude. We do not need people around us when we pray or read the Bible. In fact, their presence could be distracting and detrimental to our growth. But there is one discipline that cannot be done in private. That is joining a church and becoming a part of a Christian family.

But like every family, the church has its share of dysfunction.

Methodist minister William Willimon once complained, "The Bishop keeps sending me to the wrong church." Within the Methodist tradition, pastors are reassigned every few years. Each time Willimon received a new appointment, he thought, "Finally the Bishop got it right. Now I will be able to serve at a real church where the people are committed, generous and cooperative." Within months, however, Willimon would be shaking his head. "He did it to me again. He sent me to the wrong church. The people here are just like the ones that I left."

The perfect church has yet to be found. Every congregation is composed of flawed people struggling to follow Jesus. Little wonder that many want no part of it. And yet joining a church family is part of discipleship. Paul teaches that when we become believers, we automatically are part of the Body of Christ, "You are no longer foreigners and aliens, but fellow citizens with God's people and members of God's household." (Ephesians 2:19)

Many people consider church to be optional. "I am spiritual, but not religious" is a common claim. This is code for, "I believe in God, but

I do not attend worship services." Others contend, "I can worship God out on the golf course just as well as sitting in a pew." Perhaps. And yet, if you want milk you go to a cow and not to a chicken. The church exists to help people know God. That is not a priority for golf courses, although God's name is regularly invoked on the links, especially after hitting a tee shot into the water hazard.

Avoiding worship is not a recent phenomenon. It is as old as the church itself. The book of Hebrews admonishes, "Let us not give up meeting together, as some are in the habit of doing." (Hebrews 10:25) Apparently there were golf courses and fishing holes in the first century!

C.S. Lewis's "Screwtape Letters" is a fictional collection of letters from a senior demon to a junior. Uncle Screwtape advises his nephew Wormwood that the church is one of the best tools that their Father in Hell uses to lure people away from God. All Wormwood needs to do is point out to his charge how hypocritical, unkempt and backward the worshippers are, not to mention the boring preacher and off-key the soloist. If Wormwood did that, the battle would be nearly won. The Enemy uses the church in his war against God's people!

German theologian and martyr Dietrich Bonhoeffer was a strong advocate for the local church. He loved the community of faith and wrote a book on the subject called "Life Together." Bonhoeffer regarded the fellowship as a precious gift from God. But he was no Pollyanna. He knew how flawed the church and its members were. In fact, he believed the sooner that new believers accepted this reality the better. It was best if they were quickly disillusioned of any fantasy of the church as a place where everyone loves Jesus and gets along famously. He wrote, "He who loves his dream of a community more than the Christian community itself becomes a destroyer of the latter."[51] Those with an idealized vision of the church will inevitably be disappointed. Church behavior can be heartbreaking. This can lead to a sense of betrayal which morphs the idealist into an enemy of the church. Many disillusioned souls leave the church and proceed to lob verbal grenades at the fakes and frauds that make up the Body of Christ.

Despite its failures, Christ loves the church. Christ died for the church. Christ uses the church. It is none other than the Body of Christ on earth. The church is the primary vehicle through which God works in the world.

What makes the church so special? Why should a believer be part of a church, despite its many imperfections? What does it offer that can help us on our spiritual and life journey? What does it bring to the table that we cannot find on our own?

"The mistaken belief that a person must 'clean up' his or her own life in order to merit God's presence is not Christianity. This means, though, that the church will be filled with immature and broken people who still have a long way to go emotionally, morally, and spiritually. As the saying has it: "The church is a hospital for sinners, not a museum for saints."

Tim Keller

Traditionally the church has been understood to have four purposes, or ministries. They include:

- Worship
- Education
- Fellowship
- Service and Evangelism

---

[51] Bonhoeffer, Dietrich *Life Together* (New York: Harper & Row, 1954) p. 27.

Together these ministries offer invaluable assistance in our pilgrimage to know God better and be transformed into the likeness of Christ.

Worship

Corporate worship is the church's first and foremost ministry As mentioned in the Preface, St. Augustine observed that "Our hearts are unquiet until they find rest in you, O God." We all long for what C. S. Lewis described as "I know not what." The church's worship ministry is designed to help people make this connection, to facilitate an encounter with God.

Although God is omnipresent - that is, everywhere - he is never more active and speaking more directly than when his people gather for worship. God uses and speaks through the music, silence, prayers, scripture, sermon and ordinances. Because of this, a follower of Jesus makes it a priority to worship in God's house every week. God established this rhythm at creation when he set aside one day a week for rest and worship. It is unlikely that a believer will make much spiritual progress without regular worship.

And yet, it is not enough to merely show up. It is equally important that we arrive with the right attitude and appropriate spirit. It does little good to sit in the pew for an hour if we come with a surely attitude, expecting the worst or demanding the best. Many worshippers are self-appointed reviewers, critiquing the music, facility and sermon. How many families have chewed on roast preacher for Sunday dinner?

Hebrews calls upon us to "draw near to God with a sincere heart." (Hebrews 10:22) Whether or not we receive blessing is less dependent on how well the choir sings, the organist plays, and the pastor preaches than on the kind of heart we bring. God can speak through a wheezing organ, a dusty sermon, and squeaky soprano.

How much better it would be if we came with a spirit of expectation and attentiveness. If we really believed that God were present and speaking, we would be sitting on the edge of our seats listening and standing on our tiptoes looking for it. Those who do will rarely be disappointed.

Worship is important because it is the primary place where we encounter God.

Education

The second purpose of the church is education. As disciples we are to grow in our faith. Hebrews admonishes, "Let us leave the elementary teachings about Christ and go on to maturity." (Hebrews 6:1) An apprentice of Jesus is on a never-ending quest to learn more about the Bible, theology, church history, spiritual disciplines and living the Christian life. We will never make much progress in these areas by ourselves. A comprehensive Christian education program will include Sunday School classes, small group gatherings and periodic seminars. Those who do not take advantage of these opportunities continue to dine on spiritual baby food rather than meat and potatoes of the Gospel.

Jesus esteemed education. He was commonly called Rabbi, which means "Teacher." The Gospels note that teaching, along with preaching and healing comprised the three legs of Jesus' earthly ministry. Education was at the core of much that Jesus said and did

Why is education so important?

First of all, Christian education offers truth. We live in an age that assumes there is no objective truth or reality. The current ethos is that truth comes from within. Each of us must decide on our own what it right and wrong. There are no absolutes and the only heresy is to say that there is. Since truth is personal and self-generated, no one dare impose their beliefs on another.

Christianity offers a different perspective. It counters that truth does not come from within but from above. God is the source of truth, not human beings. The Bible is the record of his revelation of this truth. It is our task to mine the gold and jewels buried within. The Bible demonstrates the better way to live.

A mature understanding of the Christian faith will also protect us from heresy. Since every heresy has some biblical support, it is easy to be misled. Heretics skillfully twist the Bible to say what they want. False teachers are a perennial threat, plaguing even the early church. Both Jesus and Paul warned about wolves who would try to destroy the flock by leading it astray. Predators still prowl. The only sure defense is a well-grounded understanding of the Bible and orthodox theology. Then can we discern between right and wrong, truth and error.

Christian education can also protect us from participating in evil. Ignorance is one of the most demonic forces in the world. Heinous crimes have been committed by people who did not understand their actions. That includes the cross. The participants were convinced that they were doing God's will. No wonder Jesus prayed from the cross, "Father, forgive them. They do not know what they are doing." In the aftermath of World War II, many Germans denied responsibility for the Holocaust claiming, "We were just following orders. We did not know what we were doing." As we grow and mature in our knowledge of God's truth, we are better able to discern evil from good. It is no accident that theologian Dietrich Bonhoeffer was one of the first to recognize Adolf Hitler's demonic designs. He understood how Satan and his minions worked.

A church's Christian education program is designed to help us grow into maturity. It offers opportunities to assist us in understanding and applying the faith to our daily lives. It is a tool that God uses for transformation. It is designed to provide instruction on how to:

- Pray
- Read and understand the Bible
- Understand theological truths
- Live like a Christian

If we are not participating in the church's education ministry, we fail to take advantage of these tools for growth.

Fellowship

The church's third area of ministry is fellowship. A fellowship ministry is one of building relationships. We are meant to make connections with one another, not just pop in and out of worship. What does fellowship offer?

Support in times of crisis

No one escapes hard times. Such dark days are made easier if we have the support of a church family. Scripture calls on us to "bear one another's burdens" and to "encourage one another." In most churches, people rally in times of crisis. Meals, cards, calls, visits and prayers are showered on those that are hurting and in need. These are an immeasurable blessing to those who are in pain. One good thing about a serious illness is the realization of how much we are loved and cared for!

Good times together

Fellowship has a lighter side. It includes getting together for fun. Such times build relationships. This does not happen enough. For many church people, the only time they interact with one another is at Sunday worship and committee meetings. Life together includes gathering to enjoy one another's company. One church takes fellowship so "seriously" that they have a standing committee called "The Ministry of Fun." They offer a regular calendar of potlucks, game nights, picnics and baseball outings. Maybe they are on to something.

The story is told of an elderly widow who was faithful about worshipping every Sunday, even though it was difficult in her advanced years. Someone asked her what she found so meaningful that would bring her out come out rain or shine. Surprisingly she answered, "The Passing of Peace." Puzzled, her friend inquired why that was so special. In a quiet voice she replied, "That is the only time of the week when someone touches me."

The presence and touch of brothers and sisters in Christ is an immeasurable blessing.

Personal growth

Another aspect of fellowship is not so pleasant, but no less vital. This is the opportunity to grow in patience and maturity.

Church people can be critical, manipulative or needy. As one pastor quipped, "If you are going to be the light of the world, you will attract some bugs." There are people in every church that can be annoying, irritating or hurtful.

Ironically, these people offer us the greatest opportunity for growth.

In the early years of the monastic movement, one monastery was cursed with a cantankerous monk. He was quarrelsome, negative and complaining. No one could get along with this brother. But one day he left to join another house. The monks breathed a collective sigh of relief. But St. Benedict pursued him on horseback and persuaded him to return. The monks were dismayed and upset. Why would he do such a thing? Benedict explained, "Because he alone can teach you how to be patient, forgiving and self-controlled."

The church I served in Pittsburgh had a family that I will call the Smiths. The Smiths were as sweet and devout as anyone, but a cloud followed them everywhere. They lurched from one crisis to another. The lights would get shut-off, their car would break down, or a driver's license would get suspended. They were a black hole of need. After yet another rescue mission by the church, the Pastor Emeritus, Dr. Robert Selby, told me, "Every church needs a Smith family." He was right. How are we ever going to become generous, forbearing and kind without exercising these muscles?

When we find ourselves bugged by another person, we can use that as a trigger to pray. We offer a prayer of intercession that the brother or sister might be healed of their affliction. We also pray for ourselves, asking that Jesus might grant us the grace of patience and peace to deal with this difficult personality.[52]

Evangelism and Service

We receive a great deal from the church. It offers us ministries of worship, education and fellowship. And yet we join a church not just to get, but also to give.

---

[52] Ibid. p. 63, 100 – 103.

The church exists to serve those outside its membership. Throughout history, the church has fed the poor, advocated for the oppressed, and built hospitals and schools. Christians fought for the abolition of slavery and worked for racial reconciliation. Relief organizations such as Habitat for Humanity, the Salvation Army and World Vision are built on a Christian foundation. Local churches host homeless shelters, sponsor food pantries and engage in prison ministries. Service to others is at the heart of a church's ministry.

Unfortunately, a consumerist mentality reigns for many when it comes to choosing a church. The selection is determined by which one offers the most. Where is the best music? Who has a dynamic and charismatic preacher? Which sermons are the shortest and funniest? Which has the most comprehensive children's program and the most convenient parking? What church will serve *me* the best?

Although it is important to be in a church where we are fed, God has bigger fish to fry than our personal preferences and comfort. There is a job to be done, a world to be saved, and a kingdom to be built. God needs us for this great task. Therefore the primary question ought not to be "Where is the best church for me?" but "Where can my gifts be best used? Where I am, I needed most?"

One of the ways we serve the world is through evangelism. Jesus relies on us to be his ambassadors and advocates. He needs us to witness to the goodness of God. One of the simplest and most effective evangelistic methods was developed by Dr. Gil Bilzekian, a theologian and visionary for Willow Creek Church in Barrington, Illinois. He offers four simple steps. First, make friends with an unbeliever. Do the kinds of things friends do together. Second, pray for that person and for an opportunity to share the gospel with him or her. Third, wait. Fourth, when the friend raises a religious question or encounters a crisis, share the gospel message and what Jesus has done.

Another effective "tool" of evangelism is to be persons of such integrity, character, and winsomeness that people are drawn to us and the Gospel. This is the "Divine Conspiracy" of which Dallas Willard wrote. An "allure of gentleness" is what Jesus modeled and made him attractive. Jesus did not attract people to him despite his gentleness, but because of it.[53] A follower of Jesus does the same. He not only says and does Jesus-things but performs them in a Jesus-way. The way we live our lives is a form of evangelism. As Francis of Assisi said, "Preach the gospel always. If necessary, use words."

The road of discipleship passes through the local church. Though imperfect, it offers rich resources to pilgrims following the way of Jesus.

For further reading:

Dietrich Bonhoeffer, "Life Together"

Dallas Willard, "The Allure of Gentleness"

Dallas Willard, "The Divine Conspiracy Continued"

N.T. Wright, "After You Believe: Why Christian Character Matters"

Discussion Guide

1. Invite the group to share a special memory they have of the church. What was it and how did it make them feel? (If the group is larger than seven or eight it will be helpful to break into smaller groups.)

---

[53] Willard, Dallas. *The Allure of Gentleness: Defending the Faith in the Manner of Jesus* (New York: HarperCollins, 2015)

2. Invite the group to share a painful memory of something that happened in church. What effect did it have on them? Can they think of instances when someone left the church over a similar hurt?

3. Point out that the church is composed of imperfect people. It is not a museum of flawless saints, but a hospital for the wounded. Share the Bonhoeffer quote, "He who loves his dream of a community more than the Christian community itself becomes a destroyer of the latter." What did he mean? Does this ring true?

4. Indicate that the church has traditionally been understood to have a fourfold ministry.

- Worship
- Education
- Fellowship
- Service/Evangelism

5. What grade would they give their church in each of these areas? What makes it strong or weak?

6. Worship

How would they respond to someone who says, "I can worship God better in the woods than sitting in a pew"? Does he have a point? What is he gaining? Missing? How much does the spirit of the worshiper determine the quality of the experience? What kind of spirit should we bring to worship?

7. Education

Have the group share when a teacher or a class changed their lives. What made it so impactful? Jesus' three-fold earthly ministry included preaching, teaching and healing. Why was teaching so important to him? What were some of the things he taught that people had previously failed to understand? Summarize the contributions a church's teaching ministry makes.

8. Fellowship

What does a Fellowship ministry include? Most will indicate that it provides support in crisis and loving friendship in ordinary times. Point out that Fellowship is also designed to help people grow by teaching them to deal with difficult individuals. One of the three vows a Benedictine monk makes is Stability. This means that he promises never to leave the monastery which ordained him. Benedict loathed "monastery hopping." He insisted on Stability for two reasons. One, he knew God was no more present at one house than he was at another. If the monk could not find God at home, he was unlikely to find him elsewhere. Second, Stability forced the brothers to live together so that they might grow in patience and forgiveness. What implications does Benedict's teaching have for us? Do you agree or disagree? Have there been any people that have been trials for you? How did you handle (or mishandle) it? How might you deal with them differently?

9. Service and Evangelism

Someone observed, "The church is the only organization that exists for the benefit of others." While this might be an overstatement, service to others is at the heart of the church's ministry. What is your church doing in this regard? If the church were to close tomorrow, would the community notice? What are some of the gifts that your church could offer to others, but is not doing now? John Ortberg wrote, "The primary reason Jesus calls us to servanthood is not just because other people need our service. It is because of what happens to us when we serve." What do you think he meant by this?

Chapter Fourteen
Stewardship

I once heard of a pastor who offered the following prayer before the morning offering. "Lord, whatever else we might say, by these offerings we demonstrate what you really mean to us." I imagine the congregation squirmed uncomfortably.

Giving to the Lord's work is a spiritual discipline, just as vital as praying or reading the Bible. And yet this is often missed. For example, it is not unusual for a pastor to say before the morning offering, "I need you to know that giving is falling short of our budget. We are past due with some accounts. I ask you to be generous to help us overcome this deficit." True, there are times when such a message needs to be conveyed. Staff, the electric company and vendors all need to be paid. But such a word conveys the message that we give in order to meet bills. This is a fundamental misunderstanding of stewardship. The primary reason we give is not to meet expenses but to express our gratitude and demonstrate our obedience.

Imagine a church or ministry with no financial needs. All the bills have been paid and there are reserves in the bank. This will require some imagination! Even if that were the case, we would still need to give - not for God's sake but for our own. After all, all the silver of the mines and the flocks of the hills belong to God. He does not need to receive as much as we need to give. As we give, we exercise our muscles of gratitude, obedience and trust.

Giving can be done in the right or the wrong way. The Bible offers the following principles to guide us in this art.

Off the Top

The first principle is that it should come off the top. Our gifts are not to be the leftovers, an afterthought, or whatever we happen to find in our pockets when the plate is passed. It is to be our first fruits.

The giving of first fruits dates back to the Exodus. When the Israelites entered the Promised Land, Moses instructed them that once a year they were to present their first fruits to God. The first fruits are just what the name suggests: the very first of the harvest including grain, wine and flocks. Any gardener will tell you that the most delicious strawberry and the loveliest rose are the first ones of spring. This is what we are to present to the Lord.

> *"One of the greatest missing teachings in the American church today is the reminder to men and women that nothing we have belongs to us."*
>
> *Gordon MacDonald*

Why is that? Why are we commanded to give off the top? At least two reasons stand out.

First, giving the first fruits acknowledges that all things come from God. Scripture teaches that "Every good and perfect gift comes from above." (James 1:17) Since God created everything, all things belong to him. God has generously shared his creation with us. Giving the first fruits serves as a reminder that we are stewards, not owners. We give because God deserves the credit and our gratitude for the things we receive and enjoy. Such gifts warm God's heart.

Second, giving benefits us. It is good to be "forced" into thankfulness. Gratitude does not come naturally. We have to learn it. The act of saying "thank you" in itself generates thankful hearts.

William Willimon tells the story of an avante garde couple he knew in seminary. They were free spirits who proudly proclaimed, "We do not want our children be artificial or inauthentic by forcing them to say 'please' and 'thank you.' We want them to express their thanks freely and spontaneously. Their gratitude should come from the heart." You can imagine the result. They were the most spoiled, selfish brats on campus. Not once did anyone hear them spontaneously say "thank you."

Feelings follow actions. If we act thankful, we will begin to feel thankful. A sense of gratitude is the key to a deeper spirituality, that is, a closer relationship with God. When we are grateful, we are drawn nearer to the source of the blessings.

So the first principle is that of first fruits. Whatever we decide to give let it come off the top.

Or the bottom.

A couple in our church were battling the wife's chronic illness. Despite her weakness and pain, every morning she packed her husband's lunch. One of the side effects of her medication was an insatiable sweet tooth. She was especially fond of hard toffees. One day her husband found two of these favorite candies in his lunch bag. "Boy those were good" he said when he got home. "I'm glad you liked them," she replied. "They were my last ones."

The Bible recounts a similar story of a woman who gave off the bottom. She could muster only two pennies to put in the offering, hardly worth the effort. No one would have noticed or missed such a gift. And yet someone did. This person nudged his companions and said, "See that woman? She has given more than anyone else, including the richest of donors. She has given her last two pennies, everything she owned."

Generously

The second principle of Christian giving is generosity. Whatever the amount, it should cost us something. In order for it to be a true sacrifice we should feel a squeeze.

The inspiration for this principle comes from a story about King David in II Samuel 24. David wanted to purchase the threshing floor from Aruna the Jebusite as the site for the temple, the present-day location of the Dome of the Rock in Jerusalem. When Aruna learned of David's plans, he not only offered to give the plot to him but to supply the cattle for the sacrifices as well. This was the real estate deal of the century! But King David responded. "I will not offer a sacrifice that has cost me nothing." He paid Aruna the full price.

How often have our offerings been a sacrifice that costs us nothing? Do we ever give a mere pittance that we hardly notice? As someone quipped, "When it comes to giving, some people stop at nothing." Our giving should impact our lives - the kind of car we drive, the clothes we wear, how often we go out to dinner and what we order when we sit down. If not, can it really be called a "sacrifice"?

How much should we give? A good rule of thumb is the tithe, or ten percent of our incomes. This was the Old Testament standard. But a tithe is not a rigid rule to be slavishly obeyed. For one thing, it is never mentioned in the New Testament, even in II Corinthians where Paul writes at length about presenting offerings to the Lord.

The tithe is therefore to be regarded as a suggested guideline.

An analogy might be helpful. Imagine a newlywed husband who asks, "What should I give my wife for Valentine's Day? I am trying to decide between this brand new yellow #2 pencil or a twenty-one-day cruise to the Mediterranean." We would probably gently explain that the one gift is far too small and the other far too large. An appropriate Valentine's gift is a card, flowers, candy and/or a nice dinner. The tithe is a suggestion, not a rule.

For some people a tithe might be too much. If we are struggling to put food on the table and to keep the lights from being shut off, we probably should not tithe. If we are not paying our creditors in order to give 10% to the Lord, we should hold off until our finances improve. God wants us to pay people what we owe them. It is important to remember that God is our Father, not our accountant. He is not pouring over a ledger sheet to make sure we are paying every last dime. Paul wrote, "For if the willingness is there, the gift is acceptable according to what one has, not according to what he does not have." (II Corinthians 8:12)

On the other hand, for some people a tithe is not enough. If we have been especially blessed in one area of life, we ought to be extra generous with that gift. If we have the gift of a singing voice, we should offer to use that more than the average person. We ought to volunteer for the choir, sing solos or give lessons. If we have the gift of teaching, we should give extra service as a Sunday School teacher, small group leader or after school tutor. If we have been blessed materially, we should consider giving more than the tithe. What matters is not how much we have given, but how much we have left over.

Whatever you decide, let it be in the spirit of David who said, "I will not offer a sacrifice that cost me nothing."

Joyfully

Finally, give with joy. *How* we give matters as much or more than *what* we give. This is why Paul writes, "Everyone should give what he has decided in his heart to give, not reluctantly or under compulsion, for God loves a cheerful giver." (II Corinthians 9:7) If we give out of guilt or pressure, there will be no joy nor will it be pleasing to God. Someone said, "God looks at the heart, not the hand – the giver, not the gift."

> *"It's not how much we give, but how much love we put into the giving."*
>
> ***Mother Theresa***

Some within the "wealth and prosperity" camp preach a message of giving in order to receive. If we are struggling with finances, it is because we have not given enough to the ministry. But by sowing a seed of faith of $100, God will bless us by sending $1000 back. The message is that we give in order to get. This is a misunderstanding of Christian stewardship.

We give to the Lord because we have *already* received from him. The primary motivation for our gift is to be gratitude. We contribute because we are overwhelmed with God's generosity to us, both materially and spiritually. When we are grateful, we can give with joy. Such a spirit is more important than the gift itself.

What if we do not feel grateful, generous or joyful? First of all, as a spiritual discipline, giving should not be dependent on what we are feeling at the moment. We give what we have decided to do. At the same time, someone who is genuinely reluctant or resentful ought not to give. (I hope my Trustees do not read that line.) These feelings indicate that something is wrong. Giving functions as a spiritual thermometer, revealing where we are at with the Lord. A small gift offered reluctantly is a sign that all is not well spiritually. It signifies our need to take some time to contemplate God's love and open ourselves up to it. The touch of God's grace will rekindle the joy of giving.

As we present our offerings to the Lord, let it be:

• *An act of obedience*

We are commanded by God to present our first fruits to the Lord as a way of acknowledging that all we have has come from his hand.

• *An act of gratitude*

Our giving is never to be an attempt to bribe God into giving us more. We give, not in order to receive, but because we have already received abundantly.

• *An act of trust*

We all have bills to pay. There is never enough money to go around. But by presenting our offerings we are saying to the Lord, "We believe that as you provide for the birds of the air and the lilies of the field, so will you meet our needs."

That is the discipline of stewardship.

Discussion Guide

1. What was the best gift you ever received? What made it so special?

2. What kind of gifts do you think are special to God? Name some biblical figures who gave generously to the Lord. Who were they and what did they offer? What made these gifts special?

3. Stewardship begins with the recognition that everything belongs to God. He owns all but entrusts us with creation to use and enjoy. Dutch theologian and statesman Abraham Kuyper wrote, "In the total expanse of human life there is not a single square inch of which the Christ, Who alone is sovereign, does not declare, 'That is mine!'" What implications does that have for us? Someone advised, "Hold the things of the world with open hands." What do you think she meant? How would your life be different if you held the things you "own" with open hands?

4. The first principle of giving is that it should be **"off the top."** Why do you think it was so important for the Israelites (and us) to present the first fruits? How hard is it to do that, especially in ancient Israel? Among other things, giving is an act of obedience to God's command. What does obedience, or lack thereof, represent?

5. The second principle of giving is that it **costs us something.** Our gifts can only be considered a sacrifice if we feel it. Bishop Fulton J. Sheen said, "Never measure your generosity by what you give, but rather by what you have left." King David insisted, "I will give no sacrifice that cost me nothing." Why was David so adamant about this? Pastor John S. Bonnell observed, "It is an anomaly of modern life that many find giving to be a burden. Such persons have omitted a preliminary giving. If one first gives himself to the Lord, all other giving is easy."

In a similar vein, Augustine said, "Everything is easy for love." What do you think they were getting at?

6. The third principle is that our giving be **joyful**. Where does the joy come from? What should we do when we do not feel joyful? Have you ever received a gift that was given reluctantly? How did it make you feel?

7. Preacher Stephen Olford wrote, "I am convinced that the devil has caused the subject of giving to stir up resistance and resentment among God's people because he knows there are few ways of spiritual enrichment like the exercise of faithful stewardship." What are these rewards?

8. Why do you think Jesus said, "When you give to the needy, do not let your left hand know what your right hand is doing, so that your giving may be in secret."? Is it possible to give for the wrong reasons? What might they be?

9. Why do you think the Bible says, "It is better to give than to receive?"

Chapter Fifteen
Suffering

In his sermon, "Bright Suns in Dark Nights," Gardner C. Taylor shared the following story.

Aquila Matthews lived in Atlantic City and was one of the leading citizens of that city. She was greatly gifted in music. She told once of a young woman with a marvelous voice for singing. A man who had been soundly trained in music heard her sing and said to her, "You are going to be a great singer one day." She, in her youth eager to get the brass ring, you know, to reach the goal said, "When?" He said, "As soon as your heart gets broken." [54]

We can practice the Spiritual Disciplines for years and still not be transformed or reach our full potential. Something else is needed. That "something" is neither pleasant nor welcomed. It is suffering.

Taylor said, "You and I will never grow up to what God wants us to be until we learn to pass through the nighttime[55]...You and I will never come to the stature God intends us to have unless we get some scars."[56] Suffering plays a critical role in the process of transforming us into our true and best selves.

---

[54] Taylor, Gardner C. *The Words of Gardner Taylor: Volume 3: Quintessential Classics, 1980 – Present* (Valley Forge: Judson Press, 2000) p. 60
[55] Ibid. p. 60.
[56] Taylor, Gardner C. *The Words of Gardner Taylor: Volume 1: NBC Radio Sermons 1959-1970* (Valley Forge: Judson Press, 1999) p. 138.

No one likes suffering. No one but a masochist seeks it out. But contrary to the secular world which sees no redeeming value in suffering, Christianity offers a different perspective. Our faith declares that pain plays a role in our transformation. It is a tool God for uses for our benefit and for others.[57] As Taylor preached, "When things go against us, when we are put to the test, when every nerve is on edge, when we are under stress, when we do not know how it is going to turnout, when it looks like it will not turn out right – you and I need that."[58]

No one escapes disappointment, heartache and pain. We live in a fallen world. Each of us will become familiar with these unwelcomed guests before our time on earth is over. The question is, "How can God use it in our lives? What possible good can come from pain and suffering?"

> *"I came to realize that at the heart of why people disbelieve and believe in God, of why people decline and grow in character, of how God become less real and more real to us – is suffering. The great theme of the Bible itself is how God brings fullness of joy and not just despite but through suffering."*
>
> ***Tim Keller***

Encountering God

The first and by far the most important positive that can come out of suffering is encountering God in a personal way. When the sun is shining and the wind is at our back, it is easy to ignore God or take him for granted. We might profess to believe in God, but he is like a

---

[57] Keller, Timothy. *Walking with God Through Pain and Suffering* (New York: Penguin, 2013) p. 21 & 163.
[58] Taylor, op.cit. Vol 3, p. 60.

distant uncle who we really do not know. Our lives are running rather well, thank you very much, and we sense no real need for God. But when suffering comes to pay a visit God suddenly becomes very important.

It is true that many people choose to reject God because of their suffering. They blame him for their misery. The unfairness leads to bitterness and hostility. "If God is all powerful, he could have prevented this. Or he could make it stop, but he didn't. I don't want anything to do with a God like that." Pain has put them on the road to rejection of God.

And yet while many people lose God because of their sufferings, many other people find him in the midst of their pain. Ignatius of Loyola wrote, "It takes a desert to find God." For most people, God will not become a reality until we find ourselves in a barren wilderness. Ignatius knew this from experience. In his younger years he was a dandy – handsome, rich, personable, vain, and well-connected. He had designs on becoming a nobleman with a career in commerce and politics. Few doubted that he would succeed. But everything changed when a cannonball shattered his leg and his dreams. As he convalesced, he picked up a book about the saints of the church. As he contemplated their lives, he found himself strangely drawn to their calling. The old way of life that once held such fascination for him, now felt dry and empty. He committed himself to service to the Lord, something that would never have happened without a well-placed fusillade. Ignatius came to know God in a personal way because of his months on a hospital bed. Presbyterian minister Tim Keller wrote, "It is an exaggeration to say that no one finds God unless suffering comes into their lives – but it is not a big one."[59]

---

[59] Keller, op.cit. p. 5.

The medieval scholar Boethius was falsely accused of treason, leading to imprisonment and a death sentence. In his cell he wrote "The Consolation of Philosophy" in which he wrestled with the problem of unjust suffering. In this allegory Lady Philosophy visits him and explains that he is looking at things in the wrong way. True joy is not derived from prosperity or social status, as most people think. It is only found in unity with God. And only those who have been stripped of power, health and comfort are in a position to recognize and receive this. Those who are rich in the things of the world feel little need for God. Therefore, a wicked person who goes through life with all the luxuries he could desire is, in fact, being punished because he will never be moved to union with God.[60] Perhaps this is what Jesus meant when he said, "Blessed are the poor, for theirs is the Kingdom of God."

A modern-day example of this is Charles Colson. Colson was one of Richard Nixon's most reliable henchmen, infamously known for boasting that he would run over his grandmother to reelect the President. Few people possessed as much power as he wielded in Washington, D.C. But his world fell apart when he was imprisoned for his role in the Watergate scandal. It was behind bars that Iowa Senator Harold Hughes, himself a recovering alcoholic, witnessed to him. Colson became a Christian and before long an outspoken ambassador for the cause of Christ, especially in prison ministry. Such a transformation was unthinkable, but it happened because of his painful downfall.

It is not just non-Christians who meet God in the midst of trouble. Believers do as well. Many of us Christians have little more than a nodding relationship with Jesus. We are *acquainted* with him, but do not really *know* him. We have not entered into a vital relationship

---

[60] Armstrong, Dorsey. *Great Minds of the Medieval World* (Chantilly, VA: The Teaching Company, 2014) pp. 21, 22.

with Christ. We have never truly experienced his presence, grace and love. It is not until the dark clouds come rolling in that we come to know Jesus in a personal way. That was the case for noted theologian Joseph Sittler. Towards the end of his life he remarked, "I have discovered something in this hospital bed that I have never known or preached on – the loving Fatherhood of God."

Rabbi Harold Kushner wrote a book on the Twenty-third Psalm. He shares this beloved Psalm with those enduring horrific ordeals. He tells them, "David wrote, 'Yea, though I walk through the valley of the shadow of death, I will fear no evil *for thou art with me.*' You are in that shadowy valley right now, and I know that is hard. But like David, you will have the opportunity to experience God in a way you never have known before, precisely because of what you are going through."

Reforming Us

Suffering can also change and improve us. James wrote,

Consider it pure joy, my brothers, whenever you face trials of many kinds, because you know that the testing of your faith develops perseverance. Perseverance must finish its work so that you may be mature and complete, not lacking anything. (James 1:2-4)

In a similar vein Peter instructs,

...though now for a little while you may have had to suffer grief in all kinds of trials. These have come so that your faith – of greater worth than gold, which perishes even though refined by fire – may be proved genuine and may result in praise, glory and honor when Jesus Christ is revealed. (I Peter 1:6, 7)

Suffering functions like a refining fire, burning away the impurities in our lives. We all carry sludge in our hearts and minds. Even the best of us are weighed down by sinful attitudes, habits and behaviors.

Fortunately, (or unfortunately) these are not easily seen. We do a pretty good job of hiding our flaws. They can even become invisible to ourselves! It bears repeating that sin blinds us to our own sinfulness. But suffering opens our eyes to our flaws. It brings to the surface those unseen spirits. Someone used the analogy of an earthen pitcher. Though filled, it is impossible to see what it contains. Impossible, that is, until the jug is jostled. Then what is inside comes splashing out. Much of our inner unloveliness remains unseen until we are jostled by life. Then what was hidden spills over, and it is not pretty. We discover that we are more selfish and self-centered than we ever imagined. Or maybe what gushes out is rage and self-pity. Perhaps we suddenly realize that we are far weaker, shallow or frightened than we imagined.

When we come face to face with our fallen condition, we are in a position to repent, which means turning towards God and away from our sinfulness. Lee Atwater was another politician who had apparently attended the Charles Colson School for Mean-Spirited Politics. In the cut-throat business of national politics, Atwater wielded the sharpest sword. None who crossed his path emerged unscathed. Then he was diagnosed with an incurable cancer that eventually took his life. This is what he wrote in a February 1991 article for Life magazine.

My illness helped me to see that what was missing in society is what was missing in me: a little heart, a lot of brotherhood. The 80's were about acquiring – acquiring wealth, power, prestige. I know. I acquired more wealth, power, and prestige than most. But you can acquire all you want and still feel empty. What power wouldn't I trade for a little more time with my family? What price wouldn't

I pay for an evening with friends? It took a deadly illness to put me eye to eye with that truth, but it is a truth that the country, caught up in its ruthless ambitions and moral decay, can learn on my dime. I don't know who will lead us through the 90's, but they must be made to speak to this spiritual vacuum at the heart of American society, this tumor of the soul.

Suffering breaks us, making us more humble, patient, kind, grateful, principled, strong and caring. It changes priorities and reveals what really matters. Things like family, God and service to others. Marcel Proust wrote,

We do not receive wisdom, we must discover it for ourselves, after a journey through the wilderness which no one can make for us, which no one can spare us.[61]

Suffering produces character, as you know if you have ever met a truly saintly person. The chances are great that they have witnessed much pain in their lives. As someone observed, "Every saint walks on bloody feet."

We saw evidence of this is the aftermath of the shooting at the Mother Emmanuel AME Church in Charleston, South Carolina. Seven members of the Wednesday night Bible study were gunned down by a disturbed young man. When the killer was arraigned, family members had the opportunity to speak. With tear-streaked cheeks and grief wracked voices, person after person rose to express forgiveness. It was an amazing display. Where does such dignity, such strength and such grace come from? Only people who have been forged in the white-hot fires of suffering can rise to that level of character. Perhaps only those in the African American community, so familiar with injustice and oppression, can demonstrate such Christlikeness. White America can only look on and marvel.

---

[61] Keller, op.cit. *p. 186.*

The role of suffering is to turn us into people like that.

Equipping Us for Greater Service

Suffering equips us to be of greater service to others. To paraphrase something that Rick Warren wrote in "The Purpose Driven Life," our greatest heartache, our greatest failure, our greatest sorrow, our greatest disappointment will be the source of our greatest ministry. In a similar vein, Henri Nouwen in "The Wounded Healer" maintains that the best comforters are those who have been deeply wounded themselves.

"The only thing that's taught one anything is suffering. Not success, not happiness, not anything like that, the only thing that really teaches one what life's about – the joy of understanding, the joy of coming in contact with what life really signifies – is suffering, affliction."

Malcolm Muggeridge to William F. Buckley.

Suffering awakens an empathy and compassion for others treading in chilly deep waters and walking through dark valleys. We have an understanding of what they are going through and what they need most. This in itself is a gift. Suffering people need to know that someone is with them who understands and cares.

The late Joseph Cardinal Bernardin recognized this after his diagnosis with the pancreatic cancer that eventually took his life. In "The Gift of Peace" he wrote,

Throughout my priesthood, I have always taken seriously my role as one who reaches out to others with compassion and understanding, as one who bears witness to the faith... In light of my cancer ministry, I began to recognize the unique and special nature of another community to which I now belong: the community of those who suffer from cancer and other serious illnesses. Those in this community see things differently. Life takes on new meaning, and suddenly it become easier to separate the essential from the peripheral...So often in the past I, like most of us, have struggled with what to say to people who are suffering. But since I was diagnosed as having cancer, words have come much more easily. So has the ability to know when to listen or to simply reach out my hand... Above all else, I want people to know that I walk with them as their brother, their friend.[62]

We not only gain empathy for others, but wisdom for the journey. There are some things that can only be learned in the dark places, but they are the most important discoveries. Because we have walked the treacherous path, we are better able to guide those who are following behind. We know what things are helpful, and which to avoid. We can tell them what to expect and offer encouragement and direction when they are bewildered. We can warn them of the pitfalls on the road, but also assure them of brighter vistas ahead. We can give them eyes that offer a fresh perspective.

For example, cancer survivor Pastor David Jeremiah thought that his diagnosis meant his life was over. What he came to realize is that it was not the *end* of the road, but a *bend* in it. That insight has helped countless suffers to make sense of their travails. Because of his cancer trials he was able to write,

Please remember this. Your crisis is important to God...Whatever struggle or setback you face is intended to empower and purify you. Your situation is

---

[62] Bernardin, Joseph. *The Gift of Peace* (New York: Doubleday, 1997) pp. 92 - 94.

important to Him, because He is using it to make you a more valuable servant in His kingdom.[63]

God is not a wasteful God. He will use your sufferings to be a blessing to others. This might not make it worth it, but it does help to redeem it.

Sometimes what we need most in life is what we would never dream of praying for. As Dave Dreveky, the major league baseball pitcher who lost his arm to cancer, put it, "I would not wish what happened to me on anyone. But I also would not trade what I have learned for the world."

Suffering is inevitable in this fallen world. No one is immune to illness, loneliness, betrayal or grief. These misfortunes can break or destroy a person. They can also ennoble and enrich a life. So what makes the difference?

Listen again to Gardner Taylor.

If you have been hurt by betrayal or wounded by desertion or scarred by defeat or reverses, the first thing you ought to do is to say to God, "I do not know why I have this trouble in my life, but I believe you, Father, can get more glory out of my life since the scar has come. And so here and now I offer to you, God, my wounded heart. It is a broken spirit that I am giving, not shiny and new, but cut up and in pieces. Take it, if you can use it." When this happens, an incalculable endowment is bestowed on the one who suffers. The scar becomes a center of power…Such scarred hands heal…I promise you this, if you can take whatever deep hurt that occurs in your life and hold it before God and say to him, even in bitterness, of this which you despise and this which you hate, "If there is anything

---

[63] Jeremiah, David, *When Your World Falls Apart: Seeing Past the Pain of the Present* (Nashville: Thomas Nelson, 2004) p. 18.

you can do with it, take it, and use it." I promise you; you will be utterly amazed at what will occur.[64]

For additional reading:

David Jeremiah, "When Your World Falls Apart"

Timothy Keller, "Walking with God through Pain and Suffering"

Richard Rohr, "Following Upward"

Discussion Guide

1. In Romans 8:28 we read, "And we know that in all things God works for the good of those who love him, who have been called according to his purpose." What do you think Paul meant? Does God cause painful things to happen to us?

2. Recall a time when you experienced heartbreaking suffering. Was there any good that came out of it?

3. What was your experience of God during your pain? Did it bring you closer to God or move you farther away? Why do you think some people embrace God in their sufferings and others reject him? What do you think of Ignatius' contention that "It takes a desert to meet God."?

4. When you were in the midst of your suffering, who or what was most helpful to you? What was not helpful? Were there any "Wounded Healers" that ministered to you? What did they say or do?

---

[64] Taylor, Gardner C. op.cit *Vol. 1* pp. 138, 163

5. Can you think of ways you are better able to minister to others as a result of your dark valley?

6. How are you different as a result of your suffering? What have you learned? Did it change you in any way? What do you think of John Ortberg's comment, "Suffering always changes us, but it does not necessarily change us for the better." Can you think of people who have been changed for the better? The worse?

7. Have you ever met someone who was a true saint? What qualities did they demonstrate? What role did suffering play in their transformation?

8. The church teaches the value of what it calls "Redemptive Suffering." How can suffering be redeemed? Can you think of any examples where suffering has produced a great good? Is there any suffering that is beyond redemption?

9. Where are you suffering right now? How might God use this to bring you closer to him, refine you, or equip you for greater service? Can you pray Gardner Taylor's prayer?

Section Three

Side-trips on the Journey – Questions that Puzzle Us

Chapter Sixteen
How Can We Make Wise Decisions?

How can we make wise decisions? When we are faced with two attractive options, how do we choose? How do we discern what God's will?

Imagine a young woman named Wendy. In high school a number of her friends discovered meth, with devastating results. Some died, some became addicted and others were emotionally or physically scarred. She felt called to become a physician working in the area of substance abuse. It would not pay well, but money is not important to her. In college she met a young man named Robert. He is intelligent, hard-working and treated Wendy

"Ignatian discernment means trusting that through your reason and your inner life, God will help to draw you to good decisions, because God desires for you to make good, loving, healthy, positive, life-giving choices."

James Martin, S.J.

well. His goal is to become successful in banking and finance. Although sympathetic to Wendy's calling, he is not fully supportive. He encourages her to go into a more lucrative practice. "Why don't you become a general physician first and go into private practice? After some years, if you still want to go enter the substance abuse field, we would have enough finances for you to open up your own clinic." Wendy is torn. What should she do? She loves Robert and he loves her. But marrying him would mean putting off her dream, possibly forever.[65]

---

[65] Sparough James Michael. *What's Your Decision? How to Make Choices with Confidence and Clarity, An Ignatian Approach to Decision Making* (Chicago: Loyola, 2010) pp. 1, 2.

The Bible teaches us that God will guide us. He cares about us and wants the best for us. Our decisions matter to him and he will help us to make the best ones. But how? The Bible does not spell this out.

Someone who gave this question a lot of thought was St. Ignatius of Loyola. He laid out simple and practical steps in the decision-making process.

1. Make no decisions when you are either emotionally high or low

Ignatius cautions us against making major decisions when we are either flying high or sinking low. We are to avoid choosing a course of action when we are either ecstatic or depressed. We do not want to get carried away by the emotions of the moment. Feelings can be fickle and fleeting. They can lead to rash decisions that will be regretted later.

For instance, it would be disastrous for me to decide to buy a new car when visiting the Annual Auto Show at McCormick Place. The intoxicating new car smell, the buttery soft leather seats, and the surround sound stereo are all seductive. If not careful, I would come home with a shiny red convertible instead of the minivan that I really need.

But we also need to avoid making decisions when we are depressed or discouraged. Some years ago a pastor friend of mine was accused of improprieties. The charges were later proved to be false. In the meantime it was a nightmare. The story hit the newspapers and television. His reputation and career were on the line. A colleague came to him and say, "Alex, why stay? You do not need to fight this. We know you are innocent. There are a dozen churches who would call you in a heartbeat." To which Alex replied, "A long time ago I learned not to question in the dark what you have seen and decided in the light – unless you want to be guided by darkness. In the light I experienced God's call to minister in this place. I am not turning my back on what God spoke to me that day."

2. Strive to be completely open

Ignatius advocated that decision makers be "indifferent." This does not mean that we do not care, but that we are seeking to be completely open to either option. Strive to be impartial. Pray for the best possible outcome, whatever that might be. This is because we often do not know what is best and therefore need to be sensitive to God's leading. This is another way of praying "thy will be done." That used to be a hard prayer for me to offer. I would do so reluctantly and with resignation, somehow thinking that God's will would be unpleasant or difficult. I no longer feel that way. God's will is always perfect and good. He wants the best for me and others. I can therefore pray "thy will be done" with confidence, hope and the anticipation of the good that will come.

Ignatius used the image of the balance scale at the butcher's shop. The metal arrow should be pointing straight up to zero. There is nothing weighing on either side. That is what we should strive for as we begin this process. We are to avoid putting our finger on the scale.[66]

3. Pay attention to initial feelings

Although we are to seek indifference, we also need to pay attention to our initial feelings. God speaks to us through our emotions. We therefore need to be sensitive to our instincts and intuition. Be sensitive to impressions on the heart. Which option holds the

---

[66] Martin, James. *The Jesuit Guide to Almost Everything: A Spirituality for Real Life* (New York: HarperOne, 2012) p. 307.

greatest attraction? Which one gives more pause? What is God saying in this?

Pay special attention to what impels us. To which do we feel "pushed" and to which do we feel "pulled?" There is a critical difference. A sense of guilt, obligation or desire not to disappoint will "push" us toward one option. It is the feeling of being pressured toward something. Our primary motivation is that we *should* do it. It is accompanied by reluctance, hesitation and a heavy heart. Jesuit priest David Donovan called this "shoulding all over yourself."[67] If we feel pressured or pushed to something, it is probably not of God.

On the other hand, we might feel "pulled" to the other option. This is the sensation of being drawn like a magnet. We feel attracted rather than pressured to this decision. This is accompanied by a sense of lightness, peace and excitement. It feels right and clean. To feel "pulled" rather than "pushed" is an indication that this option is of God.

Ask the question, "To which decision do I feel "pushed" and to which do I feel "pulled?""

4. Make use of imagination

In addition to paying attention to our emotions, we can also make use of our imagination. Sometimes God speaks to us through this vehicle. Ignatius knew this from experience.

As a young man, Ignatius was a dandy. He was rich, handsome and an up-and-coming nobleman. While in battle his world and body were literally shattered by a cannonball that fractured his leg. As he convalesced, he asked for reading material. The only book available was one on the lives of the saints. He devoured the tome. He began

---

[67] Ibid. p. 329.

to contemplate life after his recovery. At first it pleased him to think about returning to a career of military or political service, especially the comforts and power they offered. But after a few days, he felt dry and empty. Then he fantasized entering the life of a religious. Initially, the sacrifices were off-putting. But the more he thought about it, the more alive and fulfilled he felt. Ignatius left behind the life of nobility and entered a new one as a servant of Christ.

Because of his experience, Ignatius advised us to make use of our imaginations when making decisions. We pretend to have decided on one route and live with that decision for several days. Does this choice leave us feeling dry and empty or alive and full? Do the same for the other option. How is God speaking through this exercise?

5. Ask pointed questions

After tapping into our emotions and imagination, it is time to ask some pointed questions.

The first question is, "Which of these decisions will lead me to a closer relationship with God and to greater service to other people?" Jesus' great commandment is to love God with all our heart, soul, mind and strength and to love our neighbor as ourselves. Which choice will enable us to do this the best?

Imagine being offered a job that will be a considerable promotion in both responsibility and compensation. It is an attractive opportunity. But then ask, "What impact will it have on my life? Why do I feel drawn to it? Is it because it feeds an ego need? Do I long to live a more luxurious lifestyle? Is it so that I can boss people around? Or is it because this job will give me the opportunity to change a corporate culture into one that is more just and humane? Does the extra money mean that I can give more away to charity? Does this position make fuller use of the gifts that God has given me?" These are the kind of questions we need to consider.

Another question to ask is, "How will this decision impact those around me?" What if accepting a job offer means our family will have to make major sacrifices? Perhaps it would mean moving to an unhealthy environment or that we would be working longer hours and seeing them less. What is fair to those we care about?

The third question is, "Where will this decision ultimately lead?" Oftentimes the two options seem equally good and attractive in the short run. The question is what are trajectories that they are on? Project the decision far out into the future. What are the long-term implications?

Out in the country, there was a place where the pavement ended, and a dirt road began. It was cut deep with the tracks of previous carts and wagons. A posted sign read, "Choose your rut carefully. You will be in it for a long time."

Ignatius would have approved!

6. Test the spirits by consulting others

Another set of eyes can offer a fresh perspective. Certainly one of the ways that God speaks, and guides is through the lips of others. Make use of this resource.

The first person to consult is "our best self." What would our best self tell us to do? What would we tell another person who was in our situation? On our deathbed, what decision would we have hoped to have made?

The second person to consult is a wise and mature mentor. We do not want to indiscriminately ask a wide variety of people. That will only lead to confusion. Instead seek out persons with the gift of discernment. God often guides through mature believers.

The third person to consult is Jesus himself. Have an imaginary conversation with him. Tell Jesus, "This is what I have decided to do. What do you think?" Sit quietly and listen to what He says.

7. Make a list of pros and cons

If no clear guidance has been offered after going through these exercises, make a list of the pros and cons of each option. Then read over the list several times until certain items begin to emerge or shimmer. What is God saying to us in this?

The right decision will always have a sense of "rightness" about it. This is true even if the decision is difficult or frightening. That sense of rightness is the Holy Spirit's confirmation of our decision.

Chances are we will never be 100% convinced that we have made the right decision. Generally there will always be an element of uncertainty and doubt. For example, I have only had about 75% certainty when making the most important decisions of my life. About 25% of my heart was saying, "I'm not sure about this." This is where faith comes in. Although never perfectly convinced, I have sensed enough of God's leading that I could trust that this was the way to go. He has never led me astray. And even if I choose wrong, I am confident that somehow, he will make it apparent to me. Perhaps a door will suddenly close or open, calling me to revisit my decision.

Sometimes after all of this we still have no sense of God's guidance. That might be an indication that God is perfectly content with either decision. If I tell my children to stay in the back yard, that is all I really care about. It does not matter to me what they play. Volleyball, tag, or croquet are all the same to me. And so it is with God when it comes to many of our decisions. Sometimes God's will is that *we* decide what to do. After all, God wants us to grow into maturity so that we can know and do the right things without being told directly. That is certainly what I want for my children. God desires no less for his own.

For further reading:

James Martin, "The Jesuit Guide to Almost Everything" (Chapter 12: "What Should I Do?")

J. Michael Sparough, "What's Your Decision?"

Addendum
The Wesley Quadrilateral

Another useful tool for decision making is the Wesley Quadrilateral. John Wesley taught that when trying to determine God's truth on a subject, especially one in which there is considerable ambiguity, we need to take four matters into consideration.

1. Scripture

What is the clearest teaching of scripture on this issue? This does not mean that we can "cherry pick" certain verses to support a certain position. Instead, we must be sure to take all of scripture into account.

2. Tradition

Tradition refers to the collective wisdom of the church over the ages. What have the best theologians written on the topic? What are the doctrines of the church? What have the various councils determined? We do not need to reinvent the wheel. There are very few issues with which the church has not already wrestled.

3. Experience

Experience refers to all knowledge that is outside of scripture and tradition. It includes the discoveries of the natural sciences such as biology, chemistry and physics. It also includes the best thinking of the social sciences such as history, sociology, and psychology. Experience also refers to our personal experiences or encounters on the subject. Cautionary note: Personal experience often carries the greatest weight in our decision making. The temptation is to make all the other factors line up with our experience.

4. Reason

After listening to scripture, tradition and experience we use our reason to determine what we believe to be God's truth. For Wesley, scripture carries the most weight, followed by tradition and then experience.

This process is not fool proof. But it is also a helpful tool to assess God's truth on what are often perplexing issues of the day.

Discussion Guide

1. The Meyers/Briggs personality test assesses, among other things, whether a person finds it easy or difficult to make choices. How easy is it for you to:

- Choose a flavor at Baskin Robbins

- Decide on a major in high school or college

- Where to live

- Whether to buy a house or not

- Whether to marry

2. What did your ease or difficulty reveal about you? What process did you use to make the decision?

3. What advice would you give Wendy? Sometimes what is most helpful is not to tell a person what to do, but to suggest a process for deciding.

4. How do you feel when someone gives you advice, either asked for or not?

5. Have each person think of a significant decision he or she is facing either right now or in the future.

6. Invite them to retire to a quiet spot for fifteen minutes to use the tools for decision making outlined in the chapter. These include:

- Striving to be completely open

- Paying attention to initial feelings

- Using one's imagination to try out both alternatives

- Asking pointed questions about our motives and the impact of this decision on others

- Using our imagination, talk with this about Jesus or a respected friend

- If no answer emerges, make a list of pros and cons. Examine the list. Which items seem to stand out or "shimmer"?

7. Alternatively: Think of a major political or social issue. Use the Wesley Quadrilateral to seek God's truth on the matter.

Chapter Seventeen
How Can We Discover God's Will for Our Lives?

When I enrolled as a freshman at Kalamazoo College, I discovered that my classmates fell into one of three categories. About 40% were pre-med. Another 40% were pre-law. The remaining 20% were pre-I don't have a clue. I was a member of the third club. I renewed my membership each fall until graduation. I needed a roadmap to figure out what to do with my life. If only there had been an instruction manual to guide me in the process. I hardly knew where to begin.

I have good news for those going through my struggle. Help is available in the form of some tools that will assist us in discovering God's will for our lives. Young adults who are confused about the trajectory of their lives will find them to be especially useful.

First hear these words from the Prophet Jeremiah.

"For I know the plans I have for you," declares the Lord, "plans to prosper you and not to harm you, plans to give you hope and a future." (Jeremiah 29:11)

That should lift our chins, straighten our backs and square up our shoulders. God has a plan for our lives! We were created to be and do something special. Certain things will not be accomplished unless we do them. Our lives have a calling. We are not an accident or a mistake. Our existence has meaning and purpose. We were born for a reason.

And there is more. Not only has God *created* us for something special, but he has also *equipped* us for that task. He has endowed us with certain talents and abilities, special skills and aptitudes. Each and every one of us has unique competencies. The Apostle Paul, who was the church's first great evangelist and theologian, described these as Spiritual Gifts.

*Now to **each one** the manifestation of the Spirit is given for the common good. (I Corinthians 12:7)*

Discovering God's plan for our lives as well as our spiritual gifts are the secrets to a rich and fulfilling life.

The movie "City Slickers" features a scene between Curly, the grizzled cowboy played by Jack Palance, and Mitch, the quintessential urban male, played by Billy Crystal. The dialogue unfolds as follows.

Curly: "Do you know what the secret of life is?" He holds up one finger.

Mitch: "Your finger?"

Curly: "One thing. Just one thing. You stick with that and the rest doesn't matter at all."

Mitch: "But what is that one thing?

Curly: "That is what you have to find out"

And that is what we have to find out. Our task is to discover that one thing for which we were created. The question is, "How?" How do we find that one thing? How can we know what we are meant to be and do? How can we discern God's will for our lives?

Some people have never struggled with these questions. They have known from an early age what they were meant to be. That includes those to whom God has clearly spoken. Moses heard the voice in the burning bush which commissioned him to go to Pharaoh and announce, "Let my people go!" There was no doubting of God's will for him! Jeremiah had a similar experience. As a young boy, God spoke to him and said, "Today I appoint you over nations and kingdoms to uproot and tear down, to destroy and overthrow, to build and to plant." No ambiguity there! On the Damascus Road the Apostle Paul was struck down and blinded as Jesus called him to take the Gospel to the Gentiles. None of these individuals had to wrestle with uncertainty. God made his will for them perfectly clear.

But what about the rest of us? We have never seen a burning bush or walked the Damascus Road. For us discovering God's will can be a challenge. It calls for careful listening, because God's call generally comes in a quiet, gentle voice. If we do not pay attention, we might miss it. But though the call might be subtle, it is no less real. The question is "How can we hear it?"

"We tend to think that if we desire something, it is probably something we ought not to want or have. But think about it: without desire we would never get up in the morning. We would never have ventured beyond the front door. We would never have read a book or learned something new. No desire means no life, no growth, no change. Desire is what makes crocuses push up through the late-winter soil. Desire is energy, the energy of creativity, the energy of life itself. So let's not be too hard on desire."

Margaret Silf

Deepest Desires

Ignatius of Loyola taught the importance of paying attention to our deepest desires as a way of discerning God's will. His great discovery was that God speaks through our feelings and emotions. This is contrary to the way many people think. In some circles feelings and emotions are suspect. Calvin, for example, taught that our emotions cannot be trusted because they have been contaminated by our sinful nature. Ignatius thought differently. From personal experience he concluded that we can trust our inner life. Many stirrings in our heart come directly from God. Ideas that pop into our heads and passions that impress themselves on our hearts are often from above. We therefore need to pay attention to what is happening inside of us.

In particular, Ignatius taught that the key to knowing God's will for our lives is by discovering our Deepest Desires. We are to give ear to the longings of our hearts. These are not superficial or transient wishes for the latest television, a B.M.W., or condo on Fifth Avenue. Holy desires are different from surface wants.[68] Ignatius has in mind the deep desire that stays with us throughout our lives.

For example, as a boy I was moved by the tales of a missionary to the Philippines who spoke at our church. If it is possible for an eleven-year old to experience the stirrings of a call to ministry, it happened that night. The desire to go to seminary and on to some kind of Christian service stayed with me throughout my confusing high school and college years. But I did not know how to interpret those feelings. I assumed that they were nothing more than wishful thinking. I could have used Ignatius's advice.

Why should we pay attention to these desires? *Because God gave them to us.* In Psalm 37:4 we read "Delight yourself in the Lord and he will give you the desires of your heart." We usually understand this verse as saying, "If you focus your life on God, he will give you what you want." But there is another way to read it. The verse can also be interpreted as saying that God will *plant* certain desires into our hearts. This means that the deepest longing of our hearts are holy desires. What we desire most is what God desires for us. This is the

---

[68] Martin, James. *The Jesuit Guide to (Almost) Everything: A Spirituality for Real Life* (New York: HarperCollins, 2010) p. 59.

how God accomplishes his will for the world. Desire is the way he gets people to do what he needs from them.

Jesuit priest William Barry writes that the greatest contribution a spiritual director can make is to help people identify what they really want.[69] He commonly uses the story of Bartimaeus. Bartimaeus was a blind man in Jericho who cried out to Jesus for mercy. Jesus invited him over and asked, "What do you want me to do for you?" Bartimaeus responded, "I want to see." Jesus then restored his sight with the words, "Your faith has healed you." (Mark 10:46-52) Barry points out that Jesus asked the man what he wanted. He called on Bartimaeus to examine his heart for the one thing he desired most in the world. This is what Jesus asks us to do as well. What do we want most?

The deepest desires of our hearts are God's deepest desires for us.

Many people doubt this. They fear that God's desire for them will be the last thing they want to do. They imagine that God will demand of them something unpleasant and distasteful. They fear that he might call them to life-long celibacy, a vow of poverty or missionary service to a third-world country. He might! But only to those people for whom this is the desire of their hearts.

As mentioned in an earlier chapter, it is important to pay attention to what we feel *pulled* to rather than *pushed*. There is a difference. If we feel pushed, forced or pressured into some course of action, it is probably not of God. But if we feel pulled to something, if we are drawn or attracted to it like a magnet, then it is likely of God. It is God's will that we have meaningful and fulfilling lives. Jesus calls it the Abundant Life. This occurs when we fulfill our deepest desire.

---

[69] Ibid. p. 343.

St. Irenaeus of Lyons, an early Church Father and Doctor of the Church, taught that "The glory of God is a person fully alive." We are fully alive when we are most ourselves, the persons we were created to be. A fulfilled life brings glory and praise to God. This fullness comes from living out our deepest desires.

Discovering Our Deepest Desire

But how can we discover our deepest desire? How can we know God's will for our lives?

The remainder of this chapter outlines exercises that will help us identify God's calling on our lives. Each of them will take a bit of time, but the rewards are legion. The result will be both clarifying and affirming. It is not necessary to engage in all of the practices, although there is much profit to this.

Over the course of a week, take one exercise a day and focus on it. Write down thoughts that come to mind. If stuck, move on to the next exercise. Pray that God might open our eyes to see what he wants us to see.

1. Pay Attention to Your Deepest Desire

- What is the deepest desire of your heart?

- What do you long to do with your life?

- If you had a magic wand or if money were no object, what would you do with your life?

2. Looking Back Over Your Life

- What were you good at when you were young? What came easily, effortlessly and naturally to you?

• What did people say you were good at?

• What stirrings did you have as a young person that might have been God speaking to you?

3. Looking at Your Present Life

• What makes you happy? What fills you with joy and makes you feel alive?

• What gives you satisfaction and a sense of fulfillment?

• What "feels right" when you are doing it? What seems to fit you?

• What are you doing when time seems to fly?

4. Looking to the Future

• If you could do anything, what would it be?

• Imagine yourself on your deathbed. What would you have hoped to have done with your life?

• What would you like to be your legacy?

• Is there something that you have always wanted to do, but never managed it? Any unfinished dreams?

5. Who Are Your Heroes? *(This is an especially fascinating exercise)*[70]

• Identify five people you admire.

---

[70] I came across this exercise while attending a spiritual gifts workshop sponsored by the Stephen Ministries.

- Make a list of the top five qualities each one demonstrates.

- Identify five accomplishments of which you are proud.

- What qualities do these reveal about you? Make a list.

- Compare the qualities of your heroes to your own.

- Do you see any connections?

- God has lifted up these heroes for you. You innately possess their qualities and are being called to become a miniature version of them.

6. Inward "Push" and "Pull"

- To what in life do you feel pulled, drawn like a magnet?

- Conversely, where do you feel pushed or pressured?

- God's call on your life is experienced as a pull, rather than a push – even those things that are difficult.

7. Personal Crisis

- A personal crisis such as an illness, death of a loved one, loss of employment, etc., has a way of clarifying one's deepest desire.

Qualifiers

Although God speaks to us through our emotions, we need to be careful not to be misled. Satan is a counterfeiter and he will try to lead us astray. The following are some suggestions to guard against his wiles.

1. Test the reality of the situation

Use common sense. For example, it is unlikely that God would call someone who has palsy or faints at the sight of blood to be a brain surgeon, even if he or she feels drawn to this profession.

2. Test the spirits

Be sure to test your feelings by seeking confirmation by two or more witnesses. Those witnesses can take many forms, but generally include such things as doors opening or closing, coincidences and surprises, or comments people make.

3. The counsel of mature believers

God gives some Christians the gift of wisdom and discernment. Seek out these sages and share your thoughts and feelings with them.

4. What is best for those closest to you?

If your deepest desire will create undo hardships for your spouse or children, tread carefully. God did not allow Abraham to sacrifice his son. He is unlikely to ask that of you.

5. A sense of rightness

Whenever God calls you to something it will almost always have a sense of rightness about it, even if it is difficult or frightening.

It might be that after all this exploration and testing we discover that God's will for us is what we are already doing! He wants us to remain as a teacher or a stay-at-home mother. This is more common than not. The difference is that we now go about our lives with a new perspective. We recognize our work as our calling, our vocation, and our ministry.

For further reading:

Victor Frankl, "Man's Search for Meaning"

James Martin, "The Jesuit Guide to (Almost) Everything (Chapters Three and Thirteen)

Margaret Self, "Inner Compass: An Invitation to Ignatian Spirituality"

Discussion Guide

1. Ask the group, "As a child, what did you want to be when you grew up?" Go around the circle and share.

2. Now have each one share their current vocations and how they came to it. Have they ever thought about changing careers? To what and why?

3. Point out that God has called and gifted every believer to some kind of ministry or service. Some are fortunate to have this line up with their careers. For others, their ministry is an avocation, something to engage in during their non-working hours. Ask the group to share their "thing" if they have one. Where did this come from and why are they passionate about it?

4. Some people have a difficult time identifying their purpose in life. This chapter has tools to help in this endeavor. But sometimes an awareness of life's meaning comes unexpectedly through crisis. Read the following story by Father James Martin.

A few months before I was to be ordained a deacon (the final step before the priesthood), I started to get migraine headaches — almost every week. After some tests, the doctor informed me that he had seen a "spot" on my test results. He suspected that it was a small tumor under my jaw that would have to be removed.

Until this time I had never had major surgery. Fear welled up within me, and with it self-pity. On the morning of the surgery, lying on a cold hospital table, with tubes snaking out of my arms, I was consumed with fear. A nurse stuck a needle in my arm, placed a mask over my face, and asked me to count backward from one hundred. I had seen this dozens of times in the movies and on television. Suddenly an incredible desire surged up from deep within me. It was like a jet of water rushing up from the depths of the ocean to its surface. I thought, "I hope I don't die, because I want to be a priest!"[71]

Ask if anyone in the group has had a similar kind of experience.

5. Guide the group through exercise #5. Prepare in advance two worksheets. The first is to be labeled "My Personal Heroes." Have five columns with space for a name at the top and five lines underneath. Prepare a similar worksheet for "My Proudest Achievements." Instruct the class to first write down the names of the five people they most admire. After that have them list three to five qualities that these heroes possess. Then ask them to list their own five proudest achievements. Have them list the three to five qualities they possess that enabled their accomplishments. Compare the two lists. Do they see any connections? Have them share with the group. Point out that one of the ways that God reveals his will for our lives is by the heroes he plants in our hearts. Through these heroes God is indicating that you are meant to be a miniature version of them. Ask them to silently contemplate this and what it means. If appropriate, ask the group to share their discoveries.

---

[71] Martin, op.cit. pp. 59, 60.

Chapter Eighteen
How Can We Believe in God?

The fool says in his heart, "There is no God." Psalm 14: 1a

If the Psalmist is right, there is a growing number of fools in our land, many more than even a few years ago. A recent Pew survey revealed that the number of people who report being either atheist or agnostic has doubled in the past seven years to 7%. Those who call themselves "Nones" with no particular spiritual identity or even interest also nearly doubled to 23% of the population.[72] Apparently close to one third of Americans either do not believe in God or have no use for him.

None of these people would consider themselves to be fools. Quite the contrary. They would look upon themselves as intelligent, enlightened and sophisticated. It is the believers in God who are scorned as ignorant, superstitious and backward. Christians are the real fools.

So who is right? Who are the fools? Those who believe in God or those who disbelieve?

No one can say with absolute certainty. There is no incontrovertible evidence that could either prove or disprove the existence of God.

But while there is no indisputable proof for God, he has provided us with plenty of clues. There is evidence all around that makes belief in God not only plausible and intellectually respectable, but also the most logically sensible. Those clues include Creation, our Moral Instinct, and our Spiritual Hunger.

---

[72] Christian Century, 6/10/15, pp. 12, 13

Creation[73]

The Psalmist wrote, "The heavens declare the glory of God, the skies proclaim the work of his hands." (Psalm 19:1) David had no idea how right he was. He observed God's glory by merely looking into the sky with his naked eye. Astronomy and astrophysics have enabled us to look even deeper. The more we see, the more amazing our creation becomes. As science grows in its understanding of the universe, it increasingly points to the likelihood of a creator God.

One of the first clues that creation provides for belief in God is something called causation. This scientific principle is that everything that happens in the universe must have a cause. It is a law of physics that each and every action must have an equal and opposite reaction. Therefore, something must have caused the creation of the universe. But what? Science is strangely silent. The first law of thermodynamics teaches that energy and matter cannot be created. But look around you. At some point the universe was created, unless you believe it always existed. But this is an impossibility. Physics teaches us that it must have had a cause. Something had to create the stuff of the universe.

It is almost universally accepted within the scientific community that the universe began some fifteen billion years ago with the Big Bang. But what caused the Big Bang? Christians believe it was caused by God. "In the beginning, God created the heavens and the earth." (Genesis 1:1) But the skeptics would counter, "But who created God? The laws of nature say that everything must have a cause."

That question exposes a fundamental weakness in the non-believing community's position. They view the world as a closed system and

---

[73] Most of the arguments in this section are developed more thoroughly in Metaxas, Eric. *Miracles: What They Are, Why They Happen, and How They Can Change Your Life* (New York: Penguin, 2014) pp. 35- 56.

that everything that exists must be a part of it and be explained by its laws. And yet this closed system worldview cannot provide an adequate explanation for creation. Something had to cause the Big Bang, and something had to create energy and matter.

The Christian community believes that we do not live in a closed system. Reality includes more than this physical universe. We believe that there is something super-natural, beyond nature and science that is just as real as dirt. Only something supernatural, outside the natural world, can explain how creation came into being. That supernatural something is God.

Another clue that points to God is the complexity of creation. Scientists tell us that the Big Bang took place in a millionth of a second. If the speed of that explosion had been slightly faster, all matter would have been diffused like mist or dust rather than coalescing into planets, suns and galaxies. If the explosion has been a bit slower, all matter would have clumped together into one gigantic blob. It would not have been the Big Bang as much as the Big Burp.

Furthermore, in that tiny micro-second the values of the four fundamental forces of gravity, electromagnetic force, the weak nuclear force, and the strong nuclear force were set. If any of these forces were even slightly different, the universe could not exist. How can one explain such fine tuning? Was it just a fortuitous accident, or was there some design behind it?

Life on planet earth provides further evidence of a Creator. Some thirty years ago Carl Sagan proposed that there were only two conditions necessary for a planet to support life. Given the enormous number of planets in the universe that meet these conditions, the probability for life is spectacularly high. But in the succeeding decades scientists have discovered that the conditions necessary for life are far greater than Sagan ever dreamed. There are approximately

150 necessities. As a result the chances of a planet meeting all the criteria for life have actually shrunk to below zero! The odds of a planet like ours existing are infinitesimal. And yet here we are.

For example, if our planet were slightly bigger the gravitational pull would be so strong that methane and ammonia gases would remain close to the surface. Both gases are toxic and make life impossible. On the other hand, if earth were slightly smaller the weaker gravitational pull would allow water vapor to escape into space, eventually leaving our world a barren desert. This is just one example of the many factors that had to fall exactly into place for life as we know it to exist.

Technically, all of this could have been an accident. The Big Bang could have accidently occurred. It could also have accidentally been exactly the right size and power to form the planets and stars. The Big Bang could also have accidently established exactly the right four forces of physics. The earth could have accidently had all the right conditions for life. It could have happened that way. By the same token it is technically possible to flip a coin a hundred times and have all of them come up heads. The most logical explanation, however, is that someone is cheating.

The most plausible explanation for creation is that there is a Creator God. No wonder Albert Einstein confessed, "I cannot imagine a scientist without a profound belief in God."

Moral Instinct

The second clue for God is the Moral Instinct with which we were born. We all have an innate sense of right and wrong, of good and evil, or truth and falsehood. These basic truths transcend all nations, cultures and ethnic groups. Virtually all people agree that stealing, lying, and killing are wrong. They would also agree that it is good to share, to take care of the elderly and to remain faithful in marriage.

Where do these standards come from?

The skeptic would say that they are a product of social evolution. Over the eons humans have discovered that such practices were beneficial for the survival of the human race. Sharing and ethical behavior have enabled our species to thrive. These values have become deeply ingrained to the point that they have become part of our instinctive makeup. Everything about us can be explained as a function of natural selection.[74]

Pastor/theologian Tim Keller observed that...

People (today) still have strong moral convictions, but unlike people in other times and places, they don't have any visible basis for why they find some things to be evil and other things good. It's almost like their moral intuitions are free-floating in midair – far off the ground.[75]

Another and better explanation is that these were placed in our hearts by God. This is clearly what Paul believed. In Romans 1 he attempted to explain these universal values. He wrote that "God has made it plain" to all people everywhere what is appropriate moral and ethical behavior. (Romans 1:18-20)

Ironically, these innate values of right and wrong, of justice and injustice, of fairness and unfairness have provided skeptics with some of their most powerful ammunition in their war with Theism, the belief that God is active in the world.

---

[74] Keller, Timothy. *The Reason for God: Belief in an Age of Skepticism* (New York: Riverhead Books, 2008) p. 140.
[75] Ibid. p. 150.

One of the strongest arguments against belief in God is the presence of suffering, evil and injustice in the world. If God is all powerful and all loving, how can he allow such terrible things to happen? Where was he on 9/11? How can you explain an Auschwitz? How could he allow a Katrina? If he exists, then he is either loving and not powerful or powerful but not loving. Either way, the God of the Bible is an illusion.

There is a major flaw in this argument.

Let us pretend that the skeptics are right. There is no God and we are just a product of evolution. We know that nature relies on the survival of the fittest. Only the strong survive. The law of the jungle is the only one that matters. Nature is often ruthless and violent, red in tooth and claw. Animals have no qualms about the stronger killing and eating the weaker. There is no sense of right or wrong or of justice and injustice. That is just the way nature operates.

If we humans are products of evolution, would we not operate by the same set of rules? Like animals, we would have no concept of ethics or moral behavior. Not only that, such values would be counterproductive. They would just get in the way of our survival. Notions of right and wrong, or mercy and compassion would inconvenient and even life threatening. Thus, atheists such as Nietzsche and Sartre are forced to admit, "If there is no god, there is no reason for love and kindness."

Tim Keller writes,

An individual's self-sacrificing, altruistic behavior toward his or her blood kin might result in a greater survival rate for the individual's family or extended clan, and therefore result in a greater number of descendants with that person's genetic material. For evolutionary purposes, however, the opposite response — hostility to all people outside one's group — should be just as widely considered moral and right behavior. Yet today we believe that sacrificing time, money, emotion and even life – especially for someone "not of our kin" or tribe – is right. If we see a total stranger fall in the river we jump in after him or feel guilty for not doing so. In fact, most people will feel the obligation to do so even if the person in the water is an enemy. How could that trait have come down by a process of natural selection?[76]

And yet we do have these values – every one of us. Where did they come from? Paul got it right. They were planted in our hearts by God. That is really the only logical explanation. The very fact that we have a sense of outrage over injustice is a clue that there is a God. If there were no God, we would have no such feelings.

On what basis, then, does the atheist judge the natural world to be horribly wrong, unfair, and unjust? The nonbeliever in God doesn't have a good basis for being outraged at injustice, which, as Lewis points out, was the reason for objecting to God in the first place. If you are sure that this natural world is unjust and filled with evil, you are assuming the reality of some extra-natural (or supernatural) standard by which to make your judgment.[77]

As Tim Keller put it, the skeptics' argument from suffering "boomerangs" against them. The irony is that what skeptics consider to be their strongest argument against God becomes one of the strongest ones for his existence.

Spiritual Hunger

A third clue for God is the spiritual hunger we all have for the divine. In Psalm 42 we read, "As the deer pants for streams of water, so my soul pants for you, O God." (Psalm 42:1) We all have a thirst and hunger for God. It is a universal longing. As Pascal observed, "We

---

[76] Ibid. p. 153
[77] Ibid. p. 26.

are all born with a God-shaped blank in our souls that nothing else can fill or fit."

C.S. Lewis meditated on this phenomenon and developed what is called "The Argument from Desire." The theologian Peter Kreeft in his "Handbook of Christian Apologetics" believes that in this Lewis offers the greatest argument for the existence of God. It goes like this:

Premise 1

Every natural, innate desire in us corresponds to some real object that can satisfy that desire.

Premise 2

But there exists in us a desire which nothing in time, nothing on earth, no creature can satisfy.

Conclusion

Therefore there must exist something more than time, earth and creatures, which can satisfy this desire.

Lewis put it this way.

Creatures are not born with desires unless satisfaction for these desires exists. A baby feels hunger; well, there is such a thing as food. A duckling wants to swim; well, there is such a thing as water. Men feel sexual desire; well, there is such a thing as sex. If I find in myself a desire which no experience in this world can satisfy, then the most probably explanation is that I was made for another world.[78]

---

[78] Lewis, C.S. *Mere Christianity*, (San Francisco: HarperCollins, 2001) pp. 136-137 (*Book III, Chapter 10, "Hope"*)

All people have an innate desire for God. It is the longing to know we are loved and that our life has significance. It is the desire to experience full and happy lives. Many, many people try to fill that longing by acquiring money, power, success, popularity, and so on. Although all these things are pleasant, they do not satisfy our deep hunger and none of them lasts forever. They are all temporal pleasures that do not quench the thirst of our souls. What we are really hungering for is God. It is in knowing his love and being a part of his great mission that our desire is satisfied.

So simply the fact that we have a longing for God suggests that he exists. It is not proof, but it is a clue.

So there you have it. The clues for God include:

- Creation
- Moral Instinct
- Spiritual Hunger

These clues make the case that the existence of God is not only plausible, but probable.

And yet, if all this chapter has succeeded in doing is getting us to believe that there is a God, I have not accomplished very much. The reality is that mere belief in God is no great shakes. James reminds us, "You believe that there is one God. Good! Even the demons believe that – and shudder." Satan and his minions certainly believe there is a God. Not only that, they believe that Jesus is the Son of God, born of the virgin Mary, died on the cross for the sins of the world, was raised on the third day, ascended into heaven and will someday return. That is good orthodox theology, but the fact that Satan and his demons believe it does not make them Christian.

To believe that there is a God is a good start, but it is just the beginning. God desires more from us than an acknowledgment that he exists. He wants a relationship with us. The God that we have been talking about is one with whom we should want to have a relationship. Among other things he is:

- Loving
- Kind
- Good
- True
- Patient
- Powerful
- Wise
- Generous
- Forgiving
- Present
- Just
- Merciful
- And much, much more

If you do not want to believe in God, you can certainly find reasons to reject him. The philosopher William James said in essence, "We believe what we want to believe and then find evidence and reasons that support our conclusions." I cannot prove that God exists, but I believe the clues he has left for us makes his existence not only plausible but probable.

In the court of law, cases are seldom decided on the basis of incontrovertible proof. More typically it is by a preponderance of the evidence. Place the evidence, the clues for God on one side of a balance scale and the arguments against God on the other. Where does the weight of evidence fall? What is your verdict?

For further reading:

Tim Keller, "The Reason for God"

C. S. Lewis, "Mere Christianity" and "The Weight of Glory"

Eric Metaxas, "Miracles"

Discussion Guide

1. Why do some people not believe in God? What are their reasons?

2. God offers us clues to his existence, but not proof. Why do you think he did that?

3. A well-known atheist once said, "I don't believe in God. But to be honest I do not want there to be a God." Why would he say that?

4. Another atheist said, "I don't believe in God, but I miss him." What do you think he meant by that?

5. Why do people believe in God? Why do you?

6. Is it wrong or a sin to disbelieve in the existence of God?

7. Paul had little patience with those who did not believe in God. Read Romans 1:18-20. What evidence did he point to?

8. Which of the clues for God do you find most persuasive? Weakest?

- Creation

- Moral Instinct

- Spiritual Hunger

9. Does belief in God make a difference in people's lives? What are they?

Chapter Nineteen
What Happens When We Die?

Heaven

"An overwhelming majority of Americans continue to believe that there is life after death and that heaven and hell exist," according to a Barna Research Group poll. But what people actually believe about Heaven and Hell varies widely. A Barna spokesman said, 'They're cutting and pasting religious views from a variety of different sources – television, movies, conversations with their friends.' The result is a highly subjective theology of the afterlife, disconnected from the biblical doctrine of Heaven."[79]
~Randy Alcorn

There is perhaps no question that weighs more heavily on the human heart than "What will happen to me when I die?" This is the ultimate question, the ultimate mystery, the ultimate unknown. We wonder about this when our loved ones pass. "Where is Mom right now? What is Dad doing?" We wonder about it for ourselves, especially when illness strikes, or an accident brings us face to face with our mortality. "What will become of me?"

There is no shortage of answers. The atheist says, "Nothing happens when you die. When we die, that is it. It is over. Finito." But most people have some kind of religious belief. Every world religion has its own picture of the afterlife. The ancient Greeks believed that at death our spirits escape from our corrupt body and this corrupt world. They ascend to the spiritual realm where all is good and true. The Hindu believes in reincarnation. When we are reborn, Karma will determine our station in life. If we lived good lives, our reincarnated selves will ascend upward in the caste system. If not, we will sink

---

[79] Alcorn, Randy C. *Heaven* (Carol Stream, Illinois: Tyndale, 2004) p. 9.

lower. The Buddhist believes that at death we are absorbed into creation. We become one with the earth, wind and trees.

But what about Christians? What do we believe? Many believers have only the vaguest, muddled and mushiest understanding. New Testament scholar N.T. Wright flatly declared that most church people simply do not know what orthodox Christianity teaches.[80] In fact, many of our beliefs have been influenced by Buddhism and Platonic philosophy.

You see this reflected at funeral services. It is not uncommon for the family to have selected this poem to be read or printed on the funeral card.

Do not stand at my grave and weep;
I am not there. I do not sleep.
I am a thousand winds that blow.
I am the diamond glints on snow.
I am the sunlight on ripened grain.
I am the gentle autumn rain.
Do not stand at my grave and cry;
I am not there; I do not die.

This does not reflect New Testament teachings. It is more Buddhist than Christian as it speaks of becoming one with creation.

Maria Shriver wrote a children's book entitled, "What's Heaven?" In it she says,

Heaven is somewhere you believe in…It's a beautiful place where you can sit on soft clouds and talk to other people who are there. At night you can sit next to the stars, which are the brightest of anywhere in the universe….If you're good

---

[80] Wright, N. T. *Surprised by Hope: Rethinking Heaven, the Resurrection, and the Mission of the Church* (New York: HarperCollins, 2008) p. 12.

throughout your life, then you get to go to heaven...When your life is finished here on earth, God sends angels down to take up to Heaven to be with him.[81]

This same spirit is reflected in the Gospel song that sings,

This world is not my home; I'm just a-passing through.
If heaven's not my happy home, then Lord what will I do?
The angels beckon me from heaven's ocean shore
And I can't feel at home in this world anymore.

We will not find these ideas in the Bible, but this is what millions of Christians believe. If we were to ask the average Christian what happens when we die, he or she will most likely say something like, "Our souls go up to heaven where they will live for all eternity."

That is not the Christian hope. It is more akin to the Platonic vision than the Biblical one.

So what is the Christian belief? What does the Bible say? Although details are not crystal clear, there are some things of which we can be certain. They include:

- Life in an Intermediate Heaven
- Eternal Life in the New Heavens and New Earth
- A Resurrected Body

Life in an Intermediate Heaven

The dominant teaching in the Bible is that when we die, we immediately go to heaven. (I am, of course, talking about what happens to believers. What happens to non-believers is the subject of the next chapter.) But there are many Christians who insist that when

---

[81] Ibid. p. 17.

we die, we go to sleep until the Second Coming of Christ. They point to texts such as that in I Thessalonians 4.

Brothers, we do not want you to be ignorant about those who fall asleep, or to grieve like the rest of men, who have no hope. We believe that Jesus died and rose again and so we believe that God will bring with Jesus those who have fallen asleep with him. (I Thessalonians 4:13, 14)

But the word "sleep" is best understood as a euphemism for death. So when Paul wrote in I Corinthians 15 that, "We will not all sleep, but we will all be changed" he was simply saying that not everyone would die before Christ's return. (Incidentally, this is a verse that should be posted on the door of every church nursery!)

The weight of evidence is for an immediate entry into heaven. Jesus said to the thief on the cross, "*Today* you will be with me in Paradise." Paul said that "Absent from the body is to be present with the Lord." The Book of Hebrews says we are "surrounded by a cloud of witnesses." All these and more point to heaven as a present reality.

But what is heaven like? It is perhaps easier to say what it is not. There are a number of misconceptions.

One is that we will float around like spirits or in angelic attire. But Paul indicates that we will have some kind of body.

Now we know that if the earthly tent we live in is destroyed, we have a building from God, an eternal house in heaven…While we are in this tent, we groan and are burdened, because we do not wish to be unclothed but to be clothed with our heavenly dwelling. (II Corinthians 5:1, 4)

Randy Alcorn, who has written perhaps the most comprehensive book on the subject, notes,

Unlike God and the angels, who are in essence spirits, human beings by nature are both spiritual and physical. God did not create Adam as a spirit and place it inside a body. Rather, he first created a body, then breathed into it a spirit. There has never been a moment when a human being existed without a body...We cannot be fully human without both a spirit and a body...It seems possible that between our earthly life and our bodily resurrection, God may grant us some physical form that will allow us to function as human beings while in that unnatural state "between bodies," awaiting our resurrection.[82]

Another misconception is that heaven will be a boring place. There is a New Yorker cartoon that shows a robed man sitting on a cloud. The caption reads, "I wish I had brought a magazine." I recall asking my fifth grade Sunday School teacher what heaven would be like. He answered, "In heaven we will sit around praising God for all eternity." That sounded a lot like church to me. I had a hard-enough time sitting through a one-hour service. I could not imagine spending all eternity in church. That sounded more like the other place than heaven.

But heaven is anything but boring. Jesus called it Paradise. The original Paradise was the Garden of Eden. That is what we can look forward to. It is a lovely place with flowers, fruit trees and people we know and love. After Paul had a vision of heaven, he lost all fear of death. He actually looked forward to it. The greatest blessing of heaven is simply to be present with God. Eban Alexander is a Harvard trained neuroscientist and professor who had what is commonly called a "near death" experience. In his book "Proof of Heaven" he wrote that while he was clinically brain dead, he heard a voice saying, "You are loved, deeply and cherished forever. There is nothing you have to fear. You will always be loved and there is nothing you can do wrong." [83]I do not know if Alexander actually

---

[82] Alcorn, op.cit. p. 57.
[83] Alexander, Eban *Proof of Heaven* (New York: Simon and Schuster, 2012)

met God, but his experience is consistent with what we know of God.

Another misconception, and this is perhaps the greatest one of all, is that heaven is eternal and that we will live there forever. This is not the case. Though a present reality, heaven is a temporary, intermediate step. Alcorn writes,

It bears repeating because it is so commonly misunderstood: When we die, believers in Christ will not go to the Heaven where we'll live forever. Instead, we'll go to an intermediate Heaven. In that Haven – where those who died covered by Christ's blood are now – we'll await the time of Christ's return to the earth, our bodily resurrection, the final judgment, and the creation of the New Heavens and New Earth. If we fail to grasp this truth, we will fail to understand the biblical doctrine of Heaven.[84]

Jesus hints at this when he says, "I go to prepare a place for you." The word "place" has a temporary aspect to it. It can be used to describe a transient shelter on a journey, much like a hotel or motel room. Or it might be better understood as an apartment that one rents. To be sure, it is a very nice place, perhaps along the lines of a Hyatt or Four Seasons. But it is still not our permanent home.

The New Heavens and New Earth

Our permanent home and our ultimate destination are in the New Heavens and New Earth. John caught a glimpse of that and described it in Revelation 21.

Then I saw a new heaven and a new earth, for the first heaven and the first earth had passed away, there was no longer any sea...He will wipe every tear from their eyes. There will be no more death or mourning or crying or pain, for the old order of things has passed away. (Revelation 21: 1, 4)

---

[84] Alcorn, op.cit., p. 42.

The Biblical hope is not that we will escape this world and go up to heaven. It is that someday Jesus will return and redeem this world. On that day he will renew and restore it. That is where we will spend all eternity. N.T. Wright has described it as "Life after life after death." [85]

This world in which we live is where we will spend eternity, but it will be a perfected world. Jesus will do for the world what Bob Villa did on "This Old House." He will take what is old and broken down and transform it into a showplace. After all, God created this world and declared it to be very good. He is not going to give up on his creation. He will not destroy it and toss it on the dust heap. He will restore it to its original beauty and goodness. As J.R.R. Tolkien wrote in "The Lord of the Rings," "Someday everything sad will become untrue."

Redemption doesn't mean scrapping what is there and starting again from a clean slate but rather liberating what has come to be enslaved...The Gospel of Jesus Christ announces that what God did for Jesus at Easter he will do not only for all those who are "in Christ" but also for the entire cosmos. It will be an act of new creation, parallel to and derived from the act of new creation when God raised Jesus from the dead. [86]

Someday the entire world will be recreated. That is why Paul wrote,

The creation waits in eager expectation for the sons of God to be revealed...that the creation itself will be liberated from its bondage to decay and brought into the glorious freedom of the children of God. We know that that whole creation has been groaning as in the pains of childbirth right up to the present time. (Romans 8:19, 21, 22)

---

[85] Wright, op.cit., p. 169.
[86] Ibid., pp. 96, 99.

If you want to know where you will spend eternity, look around you. It will be like this, only better. C.S. Lewis said that the beauty and goodness of this world are but the "Shadowlands" of the life that awaits us. New Testament scholar, Scot McKnight, says that we should expect golf courses and parking lots, gardens and homes, coffee shops and sporting events.

Paul Marshall concludes,

This world is our home: we are made to live here. It has been devastated by sin, but God plans to put it right. Hence, we look forward with joy to newly restored bodies and to living in a newly restored heaven and earth. We can love this world because it is God's, and it will be held, becoming at last what God intended form the beginning.[87]

I would love to spend eternity at our home in Elmwood Park, Illinois. I enjoy my house and have put much work into making improvements. The only thing I ask is that God would banish the Polar Vortex into the Lake of Fire or at least move my house to a warmer climate!

We can participate in the redemption of our world. Somehow the work we perform now to make the earth a better place has eternal significance. Our efforts are carried over into the new heavens and new earth. As a previously cited quote by N.T. Wright says,

You are- strange though it may seem, almost as hard to believe as the resurrection itself – accomplishing something that will become in due course part of God's new world. Every act of love, gratitude, and kindness; every work of art or music inspired by the love of God and delight in the beauty of his creation; every minute spent teaching a severely handicapped child to read or to walk; every act of care and nurture, of comfort and support, for one's fellow human beings and for that

---

[87] Marshall, Paul, with Lela Gilbert. *Heaven is Not My Home: Learning to Live in God's Creation.* (Nashville: Word, 1998) pp. 247, 249.

matter one's fellow nonhuman creatures; and of course every prayer, all Spirit-led teaching, every deed that spreads the gospel, builds up the church, embraces and embodies holiness rather than corruption, and makes the name of Jesus honored in the world – all of this will find its way, through the resurrecting power of God, into the new creation that God will one day make.[88]

A Resurrected Body

On this New Earth we will have resurrected bodies. The emphasis is on *bodies*. Most Christians do not understand this. A recent survey indicated that 2/3 of people who believe in the resurrection of the dead do not believe that we will have physical bodies. But in I John 3:2 we read that "We know that when he appears, we shall be like him, for we shall see him as he is." We will have bodies like the resurrected Jesus! Jesus is just the first fruit of a wonderful harvest. What happened to him on Easter Sunday is what will happen to us. We will have flesh and blood, just as he did. The resurrected Jesus was no ghost. His two companions on the Emmaus Road did not notice anything unusual about him. At the tomb, Mary thought that he was the gardener. In the Upper Room, Jesus spoke to the disciples, ate with them and invited them to touch him. Alongside the Sea of Galilee Jesus cooked breakfast and dined with them. He had a physical body! It is true that it was different in some ways. For example, he was able to pass through doors and vanish in an instant. But it was a body, nonetheless.

R.A. Torrey wrote,

We will not be disembodied spirits in the world to come, but redeemed spirits, in redeemed bodies, in a redeemed universe.[89]

---

[88] Ibid., p. 208.
[89] Torrey, R.A. *Heaven or Hell* (New Kensington, Pa: Whitaker House, 1985) pp. 68-69.

In a similar vein, Pastor Theologian John Piper noted,

What happens to our bodies and what happens to the creation go together. And what happens to our bodies is not annihilation but redemption…Our bodies will be redeemed, restored, made new, not thrown away.[90]

Our bodies will be resurrected. If they are not, if all we become are spirits, then death has won. "If the promised final future is simply that immortal souls leave behind their moral bodies, then death still rules – since that is a description not of the *defeat* of death but simply of death itself."

But death has been defeated and we will live again in flesh and blood. The bodies we receive will be new and improved. Although in some ways different, there will be a consistency to our present bearing. By way of analogy, consider two television sets. One is a twelve-inch black and white model from the 50's. It only receives three channels and the picture is often snowy. The rabbit ears antennae have to be constantly adjusted. The other TV is a 52-inch HD/3D flat screen model. It receives over 300 channels, not including the movies on demand. They are both television sets. It is just that one is far superior to the other. So it will be with our bodies. I am looking forward to that. I have been a distance runner since high school. In the past few years I have slowed down considerably. My legs are heavy, and my lungs burn. But someday I and other harriers will "soar on wings like eagles; they will run and not grow weary; they will walk and not be faint." (Isaiah 40:31)

We will not lie around heaven swinging in a hammock. Just like Adam and Eve, God will use us to care for his creation. But the work will be meaningful, enjoyable and rewarding. Just as God uses human beings now to accomplish his goals on earth, he will use us in the

---

[90] Piper, John. *Future Grace* (Sisters, Oregon: Multnomah, 1995) pp. 377-378.

process of redeeming the world. The transformation might not take place through the wave of a wand as much as through resurrected and redeemed disciples.

Dietrich Bonhoeffer said that everyone has ever heard of heaven has a certain homesickness and longing to be there. He certainly lived that conviction. As he was led to the gallows, he was heard to have said, "This is not the end. For me it is the beginning."

"Death has been swallowed up in victory. Where, O death, is your victory? Where O death, is your sting? Thanks be to God! He gives us the victory through our Lord Jesus Christ." (I Corinthians 15:54, 55, 57)

For further reading:

Randy Alcorn, "Heaven"

N.T. Wright, "Surprised by Hope"

Discussion Guide

1. What do you imagine heaven will be like? Where did you get this picture?

2. How does your understanding compare with the one presented in this chapter? Which is more appealing?

- An Intermediate Heaven
- The New Heavens and New Earth
- Resurrected Bodies

3. How can people like the Apostle Paul and Dietrich Bonhoeffer look forward to dying and going to heaven while many other Christians fear and dread death? "Everyone wants to go to heaven, but nobody wants to get on the bus. Why is that?

4. The book of Hebrews tells us we are "surrounded by a cloud of witnesses." What does that suggest?

5. Do you know anyone who was afraid of dying but when the time came was a peace with it? Why do you think that is?

6. To what do you look forward most in heaven and the resurrection in the New Heavens and New Earth?

Chapter Twenty
What Happens When We Die?

Hell

Hell begins with a grumbling mood, always complaining, always blaming others…but you are still distinct from it. You may even criticize it in yourself and wish you could stop it. But there may come a day when you can no longer. Then there will be no you left to criticize the mood or even to enjoy it, but just the grumble itself, going on forever like a machine. It is not a question of God "sending us" to hell. In each of us there is something growing, which will BE Hell unless it is nipped in the bud.[91]

C.S. Lewis

In his book, "One Life," New Testament scholar Scot McKnight related the story of an exchange between an Old Testament scholar and a young woman who declared, "I don't believe in the God of the Old Testament. That God is full of wrath and judgment and hell. The God of the New Testament, however, is full of grace and truth and love and peace. WE Christians believe in the New Testament God." The Old Testament professor thought for a moment and then replied, "The God of the Old Testament is Jesus' God. Jesus talks more about hell than anyone in the Bible. The Old Testament never mentions hell as we know it now. The God of the Old Testament is full of grace and compassion."[92]

What the scholar said is true. Jesus believed in hell and he talked about hell more than anyone. He should know what he was talking

---

[91] Quoted in Keller, Tim. *The Reason for God: Belief in an Age of Skepticism* (New York: Riverhead Books, 2008) p. 81.
[92] McKnight, Scot. *One Life: Jesus Calls. We Follow.* (Grand Rapids: Zondervan, 2010) p. 160.

about. After all, Jesus was none other than God Incarnate, that is, God in the flesh. He said such things as:

Do not be afraid of those who kill the body but cannot kill the soul. Rather, be afraid of the One who can destroy both soul and body in hell. (Matthew 10:28)

Wide is the gate and broad is the road that leads to destruction, and many enter through it. (Matthew 7:13)

It is better for you to enter life maimed or crippled than to have two hands or two feet and be thrown into eternal fire. And if your eye causes you to stumble, gouge it out and throw it away. It is better for you to enter life with one eye than to have two eyes and be thrown into the fire of hell. (Matthew 18:8, 9)

If Jesus says there is a hell, we can be confident that it exists. This is what Al Gore might call "An Inconvenient Truth." Almost no one wants there to be a hell. The Russian theologian Nicholas Berdyaev said, "I can conceive of no more powerful and irrefutable argument in favor of atheism than the eternal torments of hell."[93] As a result, Christians shy away from discussing it and those who embrace the concept of hell are labeled as intolerant, ignorant and narrow minded.

Tim Keller hears this objection with some regularity. His response is,

Both the Christian and the secular person believe that self-centeredness and cruelty have very harmful consequences. Because Christians believe souls don't die, they also believe that moral and spiritual errors affect the soul forever. Liberal, secular persons also believe that there are terrible moral and spiritual errors, like exploitation and oppression. But since they don't believe in an afterlife, they don't think the consequences of wrongdoing go on into eternity. Because Christians

---

[93] Quoted in Gregg, Steve. All You Want to Know About *Hell* (Nashville: Thomas Nelson, 2013) p. 1.

think wrongdoing has infinitely more long-term consequences than secular people do, does that mean they are somehow narrower?[94]

Although Christianity teaches that there is a hell, we are not sure what it is like. Much of our thinking has been influenced by medieval art. Painters such as Bosch portray it as place where the unrepentant are tormented by gargoyle-like demons who poke and prod their victims in the fiery furnace. It is a torture chamber of worms and flames. The anguish and agony on the faces of their victims spell out the unspoken warning: "Do not wind up like this."

Our beliefs about hell have also been shaped by sermons such as Jonathan Edwards' "Sinners in the Hands of an Angry God."

O sinner! Consider the fearful danger you are in: it is a great furnace of wrath, a wide and bottomless pit, full of the fire of wrath, that you are held over in the hand of that God, whose wrath is provoked and incensed as much against you, as against many of the damned in hell. You hang by a slender thread, with the flames of divine wrath flashing about it, and ready every moment to singe it, and burn it asunder; and you have…nothing to lay hold of to save yourself, nothing to keep off the flames of wrath, nothing of your own, nothing that you ever have done, nothing that you can do, to induce God to spare you one moment.

Eyewitnesses report seeing people swoon and faint. Others cried out in fear and agony. Small wonder!

But what does the Bible actually say? How does it portray hell? Unfortunately, it does not shed much light on the subject. Although it is relatively clear what happens to believers after they die, the same is not the case for those who reject Christ. Because of this paucity, theologians have constructed three distinct views. All three have biblical support as well as the allegiance of prominent, brilliant,

---

[94] Keller, op.cit., p. 83.

orthodox scholars. This means that it is difficult, if not impossible to offer a definitive explanation of hell.

The three predominant views of hell are known as:

- The Traditional View
- The Annihilationist View
- The Universalist View[95]

The Traditional View

The Traditional View is also referred to as Eternal Conscious Torment. This is the belief that those who have not accepted Christ in their earthly lives will suffer eternal punishment in hell, whatever hell might look like.

There is biblical support for this perspective.

Then he will say to those on his left, "Depart from me, you who are cursed, into the eternal fire prepared for the devil and his angels." (Matthew 25:41)

A third angel followed them and said in a loud voice: "If anyone worships the beast and his image and receives his mark on the forehead or on the hand, he, too, will drink of the wine of God's fury, which has been poured full strength into the cup of his wrath. He will be tormented with burning sulfur in the presence of the holy angels and of the Lamb. And the smoke of their torment rises for ever and ever. There is no rest day or night... (Revelation 14:9, 10, 11)

And the devil, who deceived them, was thrown into the lake of burning sulfur, where the beast and the false prophet had been thrown. They will be tormented day and night for ever and ever. (Revelation 20:10)

---

[95] This discussion of these three views is a summary of Steve Gregg's book entitled "Hell"

This position has enjoyed the support of the majority of theologians over the ages, including Tertullian, Augustine, Thomas Aquinas and most evangelical scholars.

Although the belief in Eternal Conscious Torment is widespread, the nature of hell is uncertain. The word Jesus uses for hell is Gehenna. Those who have travelled to the Holy Land know that Gehenna is a valley on the west side of the Old City of Jerusalem. In Jesus' day it functioned as the local garbage dump where refuse burned day and night.

Is that what hell is like? Do we take Jesus literally or was he speaking metaphorically? Perhaps what Jesus was trying to convey is the awfulness of the place, whether or not Gehenna is precisely what hell is like. He could think of no more graphic image of unrelenting misery than the filth, decay and stench of a garbage pit. But that does not mean it is a literal burning dump. Billy Graham, for example, believed hell to be a place where one is utterly alone. No fire and no tormenting demons, but also no friends, no family, no acquaintances and no God – just eternal loneliness.

Although the Traditional View has garnered the most support and is the most commonly held belief, it is not without its critics.

The major difficulty with Eternal Conscious Torment is that it is at odds with the character of God that we see revealed in both the Old and New Testaments. Throughout the Bible God is portrayed as loving, merciful, forgiving and just. Psalm 106 sings the praises of an infinitely patient God who is forever forgiving and restoring his people. Yes, there is punishment and judgment for sins, but it is never final. It is always followed by acts of grace and kindness. Eternal Conscious Torment does not jive with what we know about God's essential nature. As Fuller Seminary President Richard Mouw puts it, "The traditional view holds that God is loving and forgiving up until the moment you die. But in that moment, he switches to become wrathful and judgmental." If God is the same yesterday, today and forever then he must be the same in life and in death. The Traditional View has a difficult time explaining this dichotomy.

There is a second problem with Eternal Conscious Torment. That is the issue of justice. How can it be just to punish someone with eternal torment for a temporal, finite sin? Yes, we deserve to be punished for our sins, but forever? At some point the penalty will be paid. Even with our human limitations we understand that the punishment must fit the crime. We do not expect that a shoplifter should receive the same sentence as Charles Manson. We recognize that a parent who grounds his child for life for stealing a cookie is abusive. And yet this is analogous to what the Traditional View teaches.

The third problem with Eternal Conscious Torment is that it begs the question, "To what end?" In the Bible, punishment is always redemptive and never final. Judgment is decreed so that the sinful might be brought to repentance and restoration. It is always purposeful. Punishment is always a means to an end. Why would God punish someone eternally with no possibility of redemption? For God to consign the unbeliever to unrelieved agony for all eternity makes him appear to be vengeful and vindictive. Is that the kind of God that is portrayed in the pages of scripture? Is that the kind of God that Jesus reveals to us?

The Traditional View has its problems.

The Annihilationism View

Perhaps because people found the Traditional View to be so disturbing and out of character for God, a second alternative view was developed. This is a more recent position, springing into prominence in the twentieth century. This view is known as Conditionalism or Annihilationism. The theory proposes that what happens to unbelievers is not that they are consigned to hell, but to *death*. The punishment for sin is non-existence. There might be a period of conscious torment, but it is not endless. When the price for sin has been paid, the unrepentant are sent to a second death. Eternal Life is conditioned on one having faith in Christ, hence the name "Conditionalism."

There is good biblical support for such a view. In fact, one could make the case that there is stronger and clearer evidence for this position than for either Eternal Conscious Torment or Universalism. The fate of believers versus unbelievers is more often described as a contrast between life and death than heaven and hell. This includes some of the best known and beloved passages of scripture in the New Testament.

*For the wages of sin is **death**, but the gift of God is eternal **life** through Jesus Christ our Lord. (Romans 6:23)*

*For God so loved the world that he gave his only begotten Son, that whosoever believes in him will not **perish** but have eternal **life**. (John 3:16)*

Scholars who have embraced this theory include such notables as John R.W. Stott, Clark Pinnock, F.F. Bruce and Ben Witherington.

Those who hold to Annihilationism contend that Traditionalists have misunderstood Jesus' Gehenna image. The fires of Gehenna are not meant to symbolize torture and torment but destruction. What does a fire do? It consumes, devours and disintegrates. When a fire has completed its job, nothing remains. So when God sends the devil and his angels into the lake of fire, he is exterminating them. Nothing will be left of these evil beings. They will be utterly destroyed. This is the fate of those who reject Christ.

Not surprisingly, the Conditionalist View is also not without its critics, although not as many as either the Traditional or Universalist positions. The major objection is that justice is compromised by Annihilationism. If all that happens to the wicked is that when they die, they die, where is the justice? Is that all that is to become of Hitler, Stalin and Bin Laden? If so, then they have literally gotten away with murder.

The Conditionalist would counter that Annihilationism does not preclude a period of torment and punishment before the final death sentence. God is wise and just. He will dispense the appropriate penalty before consigning the wicked to eternal death.

The Universalist View

The third prominent view is known as Universalism. This theory maintains that ultimately all people will be saved. After a period of punishment, unbelievers will be brought to repentance and salvation. Those who embrace Universal Salvation include Clement of Alexandria, Origen, St. Ambrose, George MacDonald, Karl Barth and William Barclay – an impressive cast indeed! Barclay remarked, "I believe in the triumph of God. If one remains outside of the love of God, then one has defeated God."

Those in this camp point to a number of verses that speak of God's final triumph and restoration of the whole of creation.

*For God was pleased to have all his fullness dwell in him and through him to reconcile to himself **all** things, whether things on earth or things in heaven, by making peace through his blood, shed on the cross. (Colossians 1:19, 20)*

*That at the name of Jesus **every** knee should bow, in heaven and earth and under the earth, and **every** tongue confess that Jesus Christ is Lord, to the glory of God the Father. (Philippians 2: 10, 11)*

Although this is an attractive view, it is not without its problems. The major weakness is that there is almost no clear biblical support for Universal Salvation. It is a position based almost entirely on an understanding of the character of God as loving and forgiving. Furthermore, it assumes that after death there is an opportunity to repent. But there is no verse in scripture that clearly states this. The closest is the cryptic statement in I Peter 3:18-20 which speaks of Christ descending to hell to preach to the spirits in prison since the days of Noah.

So there we have it. Three distinctive views of hell and the fate of unbelievers. All have biblical support and all three have been embraced by brilliant orthodox scholars.

There is yet another theory, which like the others has both biblical merit as well as scholarly support. It is probably closest to the Traditional View, but with a twist. It is one that takes into account the character of God as revealed in Romans 1. There we find one of the clearest statements about God's wrath and the way he judges and punishes sinful people.

The wrath of God is being revealed from heaven against all the godlessness and wickedness of men who suppress the truth by their wickedness...Therefore God **gave them over** *in the sinful desires of their hearts to sexual impurity for the degrading of their bodies with one another...Because of this God* **gave them over** *to shameful lusts...Furthermore, since they did not think it worthwhile to retain the knowledge of God, he* **gave them over** *to a depraved mind.*

Notice what the wrath of God is. It is not a lightning bolt from heaven. It is not a plague of locusts. It is not a holocaust of fire. God's wrath is when he gives up on people. He lets them go on in their rebellion. He lets them have their way and allow the natural consequences of their choices to unfold. They sow the wind and reap the whirlwind.

As mentioned earlier, God is the same yesterday, today and forever. Does that include the way he exercises his wrath? Does that mean that his judgment on us in life parallels his judgment of us after death?

Theologians Tim Keller, C.S. Lewis, N.T. Wright, Scot McKnight and others, including me, think so. They are of the mind that people are not sent to hell against their will, kicking and screaming while begging for mercy. Rather, hell is a fate that is freely chosen.

Why would anyone choose to go to hell? Well, what will eternal life in the new heavens and new earth be like? Above all, it will be a place where we dwell in the presence of God. For believers, this would be a literal paradise. For others, living in intimacy with God for eternity would burn worse than the fires of hell. If a person has no interest in having fellowship with God in this life, it is unlikely that it would hold much appeal in the next. So God, in his mercy, provides for such people the only place in the universe where he is not, and that is hell.

The road that leads to hell is a process that starts here in life. Each of us has an existential choice to make. Is our life oriented toward God or away from him? Does God sit upon the throne of our life, or do we? To adapt something that C.S. Lewis wrote, "There are only two kinds of people. Those who say to God 'Thy will be done' and those who say, 'My will be done.'" What is the fundamental trajectory of our lives? This is a crucial question because that trajectory continues after death. This means that for eternity we are either moving closer to God and becoming more and more like him or we are on a path that is taking us farther and farther away from him and therefore becoming increasing ungodly.

This is the vision that C.S. Lewis paints in "The Great Divorce." In this fantasy there is a bus that travels back and forth from heaven to hell. Those who are in hell are invited to take the journey and urged to leave hell behind. But there are almost no takers. They are too proud and have been self-centered for too long. The more time they spend in hell, the more selfish they become until they gradually lose their humanity. Because hell is populated by people who are becoming increasingly self-centered, people choose to live farther and farther from one another until they are utterly alone. This is more terrifying than any vision a medieval artist might paint

Our decisions in this life have eternal consequences. That is something that all views of hell share. Every day we are taking steps that are either leading us closer to God or, as Lewis suggests, taking us deeper and deeper into the swamp until it is impossible to extricate ourselves. If our lives are divided into two parts, one that lasts for about seventy years and one that last for all eternity, which should have the greatest influence on how we live?[96]

Fortunately it does not have to end badly. It is not the will of God that any should perish. Whosoever will may come. And the bar is pretty low. All that the thief on the cross said to Jesus was "Remember me when you enter into your kingdom." And that was enough. It is still enough.

For further reading:

Steve Gregg, "All You Want to Know about Hell: Three Christian Views of God's Final Solution to the Problem of Sin."

Tim Keller, "The Reason for God" (Chapter Five)

C.S. Lewis, "The Great Divorce"

---

[96] McKnight, op.cit., p. 169.

Discussion Guide

1. What is your concept of hell? Where did this picture come from?

2. Do you think it exists? Why or why not?

3. Why would a loving God create hell?

4. Which of the four theories comes closest to your own?

- Eternal Conscious Torment
- Annihilationism
- Universalism
- Hell as Freely Chosen

5. Does the concept of hell bring any comfort? Ex.: Justice and punishment for the wicked. What difference would it make to you if you knew that evil would be punished? How would you feel if there were no hell?

6. Do you think there is an opportunity for people to respond to Christ after death? (Sometimes referred to as "post-mortem evangelism)

7. In what way does the life we live now determine where we will spend eternity?

Chapter Twenty-One
"What Is Idolatry?"

"You shall not make for yourself an idol in the form of anything in heaven above or on the earth beneath or in the waters below. You shall not bow down to them or worship them; for I, the Lord your God, am a jealous God, punishing the children for the sin of the fathers to the third and fourth generation..." (Exodus 20: 4, 5)

Whew! God is not fooling around. He means business. This is the only commandment that carries such a serious threat. Our children, grandchildren and even great-grandchildren will suffer for our sin of idolatry. We do not want to mess with God on this.

If I had been an Israelite, I think I would have gotten the message – we don't dabble in idol worship! But while God was laying it down, they were not picking it up. Idolatry remained a problem, perhaps the problem, with which they struggled most throughout their history. This is the sin that is condemned more often than any other in the Old Testament. Not greed, not murder, not adultery, but idolatry.

Let's all breathe a collective sigh of relief. That leaves us out. We might think to ourselves, "I might not do such a great job in keeping the rest of the commandments – I have borne false witness on occasion, I know I have taken things that do not belong to me, and I confess to sometimes coveting. I know that I have also violated other commandments in spirit, if not letter. I have harbored murderous anger and committed adultery in my heart. But I have never bowed down to a golden calf. Not once have I burned incense to a bronze lizard nor sacrificed to a stone statue. I might not be perfect, but at least I have not committed idolatry."

Don't be so sure. Idolatry is every bit as big a problem today as was in ancient times. It just takes different forms. In fact, it might be an even greater problem now because there are so many more potential idols than ever. Temptations abound!

What is Idolatry?

What is an idol? We generally think of it as a statue of a pagan God. In ancient times this would have included Baal, Asherah or Re. These are the gods to which the Israelites succumbed. Or perhaps we think of modern idols as bad things such a drugs, alcohol or sexual addiction. The very word "idol" conjures up images of something sinister. This is just what the Enemy wants you to think.

Idols are rarely evil in and of themselves. They are almost always good things, even very good things. The better they are, the easier they can become idols. This includes such good things as family, health, career, education, etc. Because these are all good things, they can capture our hearts. We can grow to love them too much. We love them more than we should. That is the essence of idolatry. Ignatius calls it having "disordered affections.

We can love things so much that they displace God from his rightful place in our lives. This is what Paul addressed in Romans 1:25. "They exchanged the truth of God for a lie and worshiped and served created things rather than the Creator." Idolatry is loving the gift more than the giver. Frederick Buechner wrote, "Idolatry is giving absolute value to things that are of relative worth."

Tim Keller wrote,

An idol is anything more important to you than God, anything that absorbs your heart and imagination more than God, anything you seek to give you what only God can give. A counterfeit god is anything so central and essential to your life that, should you lose it, your life would feel hardly worth living. An idol has such a controlling position in your heart that you can spend more of your passion and energy, your emotional and financial resources, on it without a second thought. It can be family and children, or career and making money, or achievement and critical acclaim, or saving 'face' and social standing. It can be a romantic relationship, peer approval, competence and skill, secure and comfortable circumstances, your beauty or your brains, a great political or social cause, your morality and virtue, or even success in Christian ministry.

Christians can be just as susceptible to idolatry as non-believers. Calvin said, "Our hearts are idol factories." The last line of John's first letter to his fellow believers reads, "Dear children, keep yourselves from idols." A Christian theologian writes, "Idolatry can take many forms. Few of us worship images, but we are all prone to put something or someone in the place of God. It might not be evil. Most of the time it is something good or pleasurable that lures us from devotion to God." In fact, our very goodness can be an idol. We can become so consumed with our virtue that we inwardly congratulate ourselves on being better than those around us. We join Tom Thumb in singing, "What a good boy am I."

Richard Keyes wrote,

All sorts of things are potential idols...If this is so, how do we determine when something is becoming or has become an idol? As soon as our loyalty to anything leads us to disobey God, we are in danger of making it an idol...An idol can be a physical object, a property, a person, an activity, a role, an institution, a hope, an image, an idea, a leisure, a hero.

How Can We Recognize Our Idols?

The problem is that we do not recognize what is going on in our hearts. One of the sinister powers of an idol is to blind us to our own idolatry. Most of the time we are not even aware that we have fallen into it.

How can our eyes be opened? There is an exercise that can help. Answering these questions will assist us in identifying our idols.

1. What do you daydream about? What do you wish for or fantasize about? Where does your mind go to when you are free? What pre-occupies you?

2. What can you never get enough of? What, when you get it, only makes you want more?

3. What might cause you to sacrifice your principles or break your personal code of conduct? What would lead you to violate God's law?

4. What devastates you? What, if you lost it, would not just sadden but destroy you? What is your greatest nightmare?

5. What gives you the most self-worth? Of what are you most proud?

Keller writes,

An idol is whatever you look at and say, in your heart of hearts, "If I have that then my life has meaning, then I'll have value, then I'll find significance and security. There are many ways to describe this kind of relationship to something, but perhaps the best one is worship.

The Consequences of Idolatry

What are the consequences of succumbing to idolatry? Paul tells us in the first chapter of Romans. He writes that as idolaters we can expect to incur the wrath of God. "The wrath of God is being revealed from heaven against all godlessness and wickedness…Therefore God gave them over in the sinful desires of their hearts." Notice how Paul describes God's wrath. It is not hellfire and brimstone falling from the sky. It is not being struck down by boils or skin eruptions. It will not take the form of floods, tornadoes or famine.

The wrath of God is that he gives up on us. He gives us over. God throws in the towel and lets us have our own way. He steps back and allows us to do as we please. The most severe punishment that God measures out is letting people go, because he knows the inevitable result. For the most part, God's wrath is the natural consequences of our decisions. God is like a parent dealing with a child with a drug problem. All the pleading offers of help, and threats fall on deaf ears. Punishment seems to make no difference. Finally the parent quits trying and turns the child loose, knowing that the road will lead to disaster.

What do those consequences look like? They are legion.

1. We Become Like Our Idol

Idolatry changes us. It transforms us into different people, and not in a good way. G. K. Beale wrote a book entitled "We Become What We Worship." This means that we take on the characteristics of the thing to which we bow down. Look at Ebenezer Scrooge. His idol was money and he became like it – cold, hard and unfeeling.

2. Idols Never Satisfy

Worshiping an idol is like drinking saltwater – it only leaves us thirsty for more. The story is told of a Texas rancher who boasted, "I'm not greedy. I only want my land and all the land that is touching it." But even if he gained the whole world, he would not be satisfied. Someone quipped that the middle age crisis is finally reaching the top of the ladder only to discover that it is leaning against the wrong wall.

The Psalmist put it this way, "He gave them the desires of the hearts but sent leanness into their souls." (Psalm 106:15)

3. Idols Do Not Last

The things of this world are transient and temporary. They will all inevitably fade, rust or perish. That includes our health, mind, body, loved ones, homes, belongings and positions. We dare not hold the things of this world too tightly. We will be devastated when they are lost.

4. Idols Lead to Sin

Idolatry has been called the sin behind all sin. Why do we sin? Why do we lie, cheat and steal? Because we think it will help us get the things/idols that will make us happy. For example, if my idol is having people like me, I will sacrifice my principles to keep in their good graces. I will go along with the crowd. I will remain silent in the face of cruelty. I will turn my back on those who I deem less important or popular.

5. Idols Separate Us from God

This is the ultimate punishment. The Apostle John wrote, "This is the judgment of the world. Light has come into the world, but people preferred the darkness to the light." Our punishment is self-imposed darkness. This rejection of God has eternal consequences. Idolatry ultimately leads us to hell, the only place where God is not present. If we choose not to have God as Lord of our lives in this world, we will not want him as Lord in the next. God grants us our wish.

The punishment for sin is sin itself. Sin and idolatry carry within themselves the seeds of their own destruction. If we choose idols over God, we incur God's wrath. God lets us go.

Overcoming Idolatry

How can we avoid or overcome idolatry? There are two steps.

First, we need to recognize our idols and turn away from worshiping them. This does not necessarily mean rejecting them completely but putting them in their proper place. After all, our idols are probably a good thing that is a gift from God, but one that has taken up first place in our lives. It is important that we hold the things of this world with open palms. By all means, use and enjoy them. But do not grasp them too tightly.

Second, we need the help of Jesus. Because we can become addicted to our idols, we lack the power to break their hold on our hearts. Only by experiencing Jesus' love and then falling in love with him can we break free. What we need is a Zacchaeus moment. Zacchaeus was a tax collector that loved money. Money was his idol. But one day in Jericho he met Jesus and had lunch with him. That changed everything. Zacchaeus emerged from the luncheon a new man. He freely gave away half of his possessions to the poor and repaid any he had cheated four times over. A Zacchaeus moment will set us free from our idols.

Idolatry is perhaps the widest practiced and yet least recognized of all sins. This is because of our failure to recognize it as being "disordered affections." The objects of our love and devotion are not bad. They were created by God for our use and enjoyment. But they become idols when they take too much space in our hearts, crowding out God.

For further reading:

G. K. Beale, "We are What We Worship"

Tim Keller, "Counterfeit Gods"

Discussion Guide

1. What picture does the word "idol" conjure up?

2. Why do you think this was such a problem for the Israelites?

3. Why was idolatry such a serious sin in God's eyes?

4. What do you think of the description of an idol as a good thing that we love too much?

5. What are some of the idols that people worship today?

6. In what way do we become like the thing we worship? Can you think of some examples?

7. Why is it that idols do not satisfy?

8. What does it mean to hold the good things of this world with open hands?

Chapter Twenty-Two
What about Miracles?

"Within some circles of Christianity, there is a cynicism concerning Christ's ability to intervene and make any difference in daily life. No matter what reasons may be given, such cynicism is ultimately the result of an ignorance of scripture."[97]

K. Lawson Younger Jr.

In the 1980 Olympic hockey match between the United States and Russia, the Americans took a 4-3 lead with ten minutes remaining. The stunned Russians put on a ferocious charge to put away the young upstarts but shot after shot was turned away. With a minute to go, the Americans clung to their tiny lead. As the clock wound down, sportscaster Al Michaels uttered some of the most famous words in sports history. "Eleven seconds, you've got ten. The countdown is going on right now. Five seconds left in the game. Do you believe in miracles? Yes!"

The game will forever be immortalized as "The Miracle on Ice."

Do you believe in miracles? Many people do not.

Certainly those who consider themselves to be skeptics, naturalists or atheists do not. For them, the universe is a closed system. There are no laws other than the inviolable law of nature. To those with this worldview, a miracle is impossible.

But there are some Christians who do not believe in miracles, or at least present-day miracles. They are known as Cessationists. Although

---

[97] Younger, K. Lawson. *The NIV Application Commentary: Judges and Ruth* (Grand Rapids: Zondervan, 2002) p. 181.

they acknowledge that miracles happened in Biblical times, that age has ceased. God no longer works miraculously in the world.

And yet there are good reasons to believe in miracles, especially for the Christian.

The Bible Tells Me So

One reason to believe in miracles is because of the testimony of scripture. The Bible is chock-full of miracle stories. In the Old Testament, there is the story of Abraham and Sarah having a baby when they were both nearly one hundred years old. In Exodus we read the story of how God parted the Red Sea as well as providing manna, water and even meat in the wilderness. In the New Testament we find a record of Jesus' many miraculous deeds. Among other things, he walked on the water, stilled the storm, turned water into wine, fed the 5,000, and healed the blind, deaf, paralyzed and lepers. He even raised the dead! The book of Acts contains the miracles performed by the Apostles.

Why does the Bible record these events? Is it just to tell us what God *used* to do? That would be cruel, not unlike a girl licking an orange Popsicle on a hot summer day and saying to her friends, "I'll bet you wish you had one of these."

The reason these stories are in the Bible is to give us a window into what God is doing in all places and at all times. They are here to tell us that our God is a God of miracles. As the Younger quote above notes, any cynicism regarding miracles is evidence of an ignorance of scripture.

One of the differences, however, is a matter of timing. C.S. Lewis observed that the miracles that Jesus performed *suddenly* and *locally* are the same kind of miracles he performs *gradually* and *generally*. For example, Jesus first miracle was changing the water into wine at the wedding in Cana. He performed this in an instant. But every day God is changing water into wine. The rains saturate the ground. The vines then drink from the soil and produce grapes. The sun ripens the grapes which the vintner harvests and squeezes out the juice. The juice ferments and eventually becomes wine. It is the same miracle, but it just takes longer.

A second reason for believing in miracles is the character and attributes of God. God is both loving and omnipotent. Those two truths give us confidence in his ability to perform miracles.

God is a God of love. Indeed, John says that God is love. It is not just an aspect of his character, but the essence of it. Everything he does and says is in love. He wants the best for us, for we are his children. Any parent would move heaven and earth to protect his or her child. God's love for us is even greater than that of a father or a mother. We should therefore not be surprised that he would intervene on our behalf.

God is also Omnipotent or Almighty. In Psalm 135:6 we read that, "The Lord does whatever he wants." There is nothing God cannot do. If we accept the claim that he is the Creator of the universe it should not be much of a stretch to believe he could heal a person of cancer. If we believe in the Incarnation, that is, that Jesus was God in the flesh, it is not difficult to believe that he could walk on water. And if we believe that God raised Jesus from the dead, it should not be that difficult to believe that he performed and is performing lesser miracles. New Testament scholar N.T. Wright believes that the Resurrection changes everything. It is a sign that the New Age has broken into the world. A resurrection power has been unleashed. He maintains that in this new era we avoid using the word "miracle" because such events should be commonplace, the new normal.

As Christians we are Theists, not Deists. A Deist does not believe God intervenes in our world. Theism teaches that God is actively involved in our affairs. He is not constrained by the laws of nature but can suspend them as he deems fit.

A third reason to believe in miracles is the many modern-day examples of them. Eric Metaxas has written a book entitled "Miracles." Nearly half of the book is devoted to miracles with which he is personally acquainted. They include conversion miracles, physical healings, inner healings, angelic visitations and countless everyday wonders. No doubt you can point to miracles that you have witnessed as well.

A Pattern of Prayer

If miracles are real, why don't we see more of them today? For that matter, why don't we see more of them in biblical times? Although Jesus healed many people, many more people went uncured. There were a multitude of blind, paralyzed and leprous people who suffered the rest of their lives. Why were some healed and not others?

It is impossible to give a definitive answer. The truth is that there is no single pattern for miracles in the Gospels. Sometimes Jesus spoke to or touched the individual. At other times he healed at a distance, never seeing the victim face to face. Some people sought out Jesus' help. Other times Jesus took it upon himself to initiate the miracle.

But in most cases people were healed because they reached out to Jesus. In Mark 10 Blind Bartimaeus offers a model of how to seek a miracle.

Then they came to Jericho. As Jesus and his disciples, together with a large crowd, were leaving the city, a blind man, Bartimaeus (that is, the Son of Timaeus), was sitting by the roadside begging. When he heard that it was Jesus of Nazareth, he began to shout, "Jesus, Son of David, have mercy on me!" Many rebuked him and told him to be quiet, but he shouted all the more, "Jesus, Son of David, have mercy on me!" Jesus stopped and said, "Call him." So they called to the blind man, "Cheer up! On your feet! He's calling you." Throwing his cloak aside, he jumped to his feet and came to Jesus. "What do you want me to do for you?" Jesus asked him. The blind man said, "Rabbi, I want to see." "Go," said Jesus, "your faith has healed you." Immediately he received his sight and followed Jesus along the road,

Notice what Bartimaeus did.

He asked for a miracle

The blind man cried out to Jesus, "Jesus, Son of David, have mercy on me!" What would have happened if Bartimaeus had not? Nothing. Nothing would have happened. Jesus would have continued on his way to Jerusalem and Bartimaeus would have remained sightless. But because he asked, he received.

One of the main reasons we do not receive a miracle is because we do not ask for one. Scripture teaches, "You do not have because you do not ask." (James 4:2)

The story is told of a man who had just been granted entry into heaven. An angel was assigned to show him around. The angel pointed out the streets of gold, the room in the mansion where he would be staying, the throne of God, etc. They then came upon a massive building, the largest in heaven. "What is that place?" the man inquired. "Oh, that's where God stores all the blessings that were never asked for."

Our prayers make a difference to God. As Karl Barth observed, "God does not act the same way whether we pray or not. Our prayers exert and influence over him." What an astonishing thought! In I John 5 we read, "This is the confidence we have in approaching God; that if we ask anything according to his will, he hears us. And if we know that he hears us – whatever we ask – we know that we have what we asked of him."

He was persistent

Bartimaeus did not ask for help just once. He continued to cry out to Jesus over and over again. He did so in spite of the crowd that tried to discourage and quiet him. But Bartimaeus was not to be denied. He continued to badger Jesus until he stopped to help. Had he not, Jesus might have continued on his way.

There is a place for such persistence. Indeed, the Parable of the Unjust Judge was told to encourage Jesus' disciples to be persistent in prayer. This is not to say that God is keeping a tally of the number of times we pray and when we reach 1,000 he grants our request. It is more a matter of determining how sincere we are and how badly we desire this request.

He asked in faith

Bartimaeus had faith in Jesus' power to heal. He believed with all his heart that Jesus could help him. That seems to have made the difference, not only for Bartimaeus, but for many others in the Gospels. Jesus said to the blind man, "Your faith has healed you." He said something similar to the woman with the flow of blood and the Centurion whose servant was ill. There are numerous other texts that suggest having faith is one of the keys to unlocking a miracle.

David Jeremiah survived two bouts with life-threatening cancer. He said that there were many things that contributed to his healing. These include the surgeon's skill, the chemotherapy, and his diet along with regular exercise. But mostly, he believed, it was because of the faith and prayers of God's people.

And Yet

And yet we know too many instances of people who were not healed. For every miraculous healing we can point to ten who were not. A few years ago our congregation was heartbroken by the passing of a ten-year-old girl to brain cancer. Many had prayed with persistence and faith for a miracle, but it was not granted. How do we deal with a situation like that?

I cannot pretend to offer a complete and satisfying answer to one of the greatest mysteries in the world. Wiser theologians than I have wrestled with this problem without arriving at a solution. But that does not prevent us from offering a response.

Part of the answer is that God might have had something different and better in store. Just because we do not receive the miracle, we asked for does not mean that God has not responded. It might just mean that he has a different answer than the one we would like. For example, the Apostle Paul was bedeviled by what he called a "thorn in the flesh." We do not know what it was, but it was the source of embarrassment and pain. Three times he begged God to remove it, and three times his request was denied. "My grace is sufficient for you" was God's reply. I suspect if you had asked Paul which was the greater blessing, a healing or a deeper experience of God's grace, he would not have hesitated to say, "God's grace."

It might be that God provides a different kind of miracle. My mother suffered from MS for many years before she died. It was especially hard on my dad to see the love of his life deteriorate year after year. There were literally thousands of people who prayed for mom, but her healing was not granted. Towards the end of her life my dad said to me, "I prayed for a healing and I received one, but it was not the healing I had asked for. God healed the bitterness of my heart." That was a miracle.

Although not all a healed in this life, everyone can receive the ultimate healing. What was Jesus' greatest miracle? Hands down, it was when he raised Lazarus from the grave. This is what all of us will receive. This is the ultimate healing. This is the miracle we will all witness.

Miracles are in the realm of mystery. And yet, just because they are often inexplicable does not mean that they are not real. Perhaps one of God's minor miracles is persuading us to believe that.

For further reading

Eric Metaxas, "Miracles: What They Are, Why They Happen, and How They Can Change Your Life"

Lee Strobel, "The Case for Miracles"

Discussion Guide

1. Do you believe in miracles? Why or why not?

2. Have you ever witnessed a miracle? Share your story.

3. Make a list of the miracles in both the Old and New Testaments. Why do you think these stories are there?

4. Why do you think some people experience a miraculous healing and others do not?

5. Is everything that happens in the world God's will?

6. Where in your life do you need a miracle right now?

7. Invite the group to meditate on these promises from Isaiah 41:10-13. What stood out? How did it make you feel?

> *Do not fear, for I am with you,*
> *Do not be dismayed, for I am your God.*
> *I will strengthen you and help you;*
> *I will uphold you with my righteous right hand.*
> *All who rage against you will surely be ashamed and disgraced;*
> *Those who oppose you will be as nothing and perish.*
> *Though you search for your enemies, you will not find them.*
> *Those who wage war against you will be as nothing at all.*
> *For I am the Lord, your God, who takes hold of your right hand*
> *And says to you, do not fear; I will help you.*

Bibliography

Armstrong, Dorsey. *Great Minds of the Medieval World*. Chantilly, VA: The Teaching Company, 2014.

Alcorn, Randy. *Heaven*. Wheaton, Illinois: Tyndale, 2004.

Augustine. The Confessions. Hyde Park, New York: New City Press, 1997.

Barnes, M. Craig. *The Pastor as Minor Poet: Texts and Subtexts in the Ministerial Life*. Grand Rapids: Eerdmans, 2009.

Barry, William A. *Letting God Come Close: An Approach to the Ignatian Spiritual Exercises*. Chicago: Loyola, 2001.

Barry, William A. and Connolly, William J. *The Practice of Spiritual Direction*. New York: HarperCollins, 1982.

Bernardin, Joseph Louis. *The Gift of Peace: Personal Reflections by Joseph Cardinal Bernardin*. Chicago: Loyola, 1997.

Brown, Peter. *Augustine of Hippo*. Berkley and Los Angeles, California: University of California Press, 2000.

Buechner, Frederick. *Listening to Your Life*. New York: HarperCollins, 1992.

Bonhoeffer, Dietrich. *Life Together: The Classic Exploration of Christian Community*. New York: Harper & Row, 1954.

Boyle, Gregory. *Tattoos on the Heart: The Power of Boundless Compassion*. New York: Simon & Schuster, 2010.

Calhoun, Adele Ahlberg. *Spiritual Disciplines Handbook: Practices That Transform Us*. Downers Grove, Illinois: Intervarsity Press, 2005.

Chittister, Joan. *Wisdom Distilled from the Daily Living the Rule of St. Benedict Today*. New York: HarperCollins, 1990.

Craddock, Fred B. *The Collected Sermons of Fred Craddock.* Louisville: Westminster, 2011.

De Waal, Esther. *Seeking God: The Way of St. Benedict.* London: Faith Press, 1984.

Fleming, David L. *What is Ignatian Spirituality?* Chicago: Loyola, 2008.

Frankl, Viktor E. *Man's Search for Meaning: An Introduction to Logotherapy.* New York: Washington Square, 1963.

Greg, Steve. *All You Want to Know about Hell: Three Christian Views of God's Final Solution to the Problem of Sin.* Nashville: Thomas Nelson, 2013.

Gallagher, Timothy M. *The Discernment of Spirits: An Ignatian Guide for Everyday Living.* New York: Crossroad, 2005.

Gallagher, Timothy M. *The Examen Prayer: Ignatian Wisdom for Our Lives Today.* New York: Crossroad, 2006.

Gallagher, Timothy M. *Spiritual Consolation: An Ignatian Guide for the Greater Discernment of Spirits.* New York: Crossroad, 2007.

Gonzalez, Justo L. *The Story of Christianity: Vol 1, The Early Church and the Dawn of the Reformation.* San Francisco: Harper & Row, 1984.

Jeremiah, David. *When Your World Falls Apart: Seeing Past the Pain of the Present.* Nashville: Thomas Nelson, 2000.

Keller, Timothy. *Center Church: Doing Balanced Gospel-Centered Ministry in Your City.* Grand Rapids: Zondervan, 2012.

Keller, Timothy. *Prayer: Experiencing Awe and Intimacy with God.* New York: Penguin, 2014.

Keller, Timothy. *The Prodigal God: Recovering the Heart of the Christian Faith.* New York: Riverhead, 2008.

Keller, Timothy. *The Reason for God: Belief in an Age of Skepticism.* New York: Riverhead, 2008.

Keller, Timothy. *Walking with God through Pain and Suffering.* New York: Penguin, 2013.

Lewis, C.S. *The Great Divorce.* New York: Harper Collins, 1946.

Martin, James. *The Jesuit Guide to (Almost) Everything: A Spirituality for Real Life.* New York: HarperCollins, 2010.

Martin, James. *My Life with the Saints.* Chicago: Loyola, 2006.

McKnight, Scot. *The Jesus Creed: Loving God, Loving Others.* Brewster, Massachusetts: Paraclete Press, 2004.

McKnight, Scot. *The King Jesus Gospel: The Original Good News Revisited.* Grand Rapids: Zondervan, 2011.

McKnight, Scot. *One.Life: Jesus Calls, We Follow.* Grand Rapids: Zondervan, 2010.

Metaxas, Eric. *Miracles: What They Are, Why They Happen, and How They Can Change Your Life.* New York: Penguin, 2014.

Metaxas, Eric. *Bonhoeffer: Pastor, Martyr, Prophet, Spy.* Nashville: Thomas Nelson, 2010.

Muldoon, Timothy. *The Ignatian Workout: Daily Spiritual Exercises for a Healthy Faith.* Chicago: Loyola, 2004.

Ortberg, John. *The Life You've Always Wanted: Spiritual Disciplines for Ordinary People.* Grand Rapids: Zondervan, 1997.

Peace, Richard. *Spiritual Autobiography: Discovering and Sharing Your Spiritual Story.* Colorado Springs: NavPress, 1998.

Pennington, M. Basil. *Lectio Divina: Renewing the Ancient Practice of Praying the Scriptures.* New York: Crossroad Publishing, 1998.

Peterson, Eugene H. *Eat This Book: A Conversation in the Art of Spiritual Reading.* Grand Rapids: Eerdmans, 2006.

Peterson, Eugene H. *A Long Obedience in the Same Direction: Discipleship in an Instant Society.* Downers Grove, Illinois: InterVarsity Press, 2000.

Quicke, Michael J. *Preaching as Worship: An Integrative Approach to Formation in Your Church.* Grand Rapids: Baker, 2011.

Rohr, Richard. *Falling Upward: A Spirituality for the Two Halves of Life.* San Francisco: Jossey-Bass, 2011.

Silf, Margaret. *Inner Compass: An Invitation to Ignatian Spirituality.* Chicago: Loyola, 1999.

Sparough, J. Michael with Manney, James, and Hipskind, Tim. *What's Your Decision?: How to Make Choices with Confidence and Clarity - An Ignatian Approach to Decision Making.* Chicago: Loyola, 2010.

Stott, John R.W. *Basic Christianity.* Grand Rapids: Eerdmans, 1958, reprinted 1995.

Strobel, Lee. *The Case for Miracles.* Grand Rapids: Zondervan, 2018.

Taylor, Gardner C. *The Words of Gardner Taylor: Vol 1, NBC Radio Sermons 1959-1970.* Valley Forge: Judson, 1999.

Taylor, Gardner C. *The Words of Gardner C. Taylor: Vol 3, Quintessential Classics 1980-Present.* Valley Forge: Judson, 2000.

Tomaine, Jane. *St. Benedict's Toolbox: The Nuts and Bolts of Everyday Benedictine Living.* Harrisburg, PA: Morehouse, 2005.

Traub, George W. Editor. *An Ignatian Spirituality Reader: Contemporary Writings on St. Ignatius of Loyola, the Spiritual Exercises, Discernment, and More.* Chicago: Loyola, 2008.

Tucker, Ruth A. *Parade of Faith: A Biographical History of the Christian Church*. Grand Rapids: Zondervan, 2011.

Warner, Larry. *Journey with Jesus: Discovering the Spiritual Exercises of Saint Ignatius*. Downers Grove: InterVarsity, 2010.

Warren, Rick. *The Purpose Driven Life: What on Earth am I Here For?* Grand Rapids: Zondervan, 2002.

Willard, Dallas. *The Allure of Gentleness: Defending the Faith in the Manner of Jesus*. New York: HarperOne, 2013.

Willard, Dallas. *The Divine Conspiracy: Rediscovering Our Hidden Life in God*. New York: HarperOne, 1997.

Willard, Dallas, *Hearing God: Developing a Conversational Relationship with God*. Downers Grove, Illinois: InterVarsity, 1999.

Willard, Dallas. *The Spirit of the Disciplines: Understanding How God Changes Lives*. New York: HarperOne, 1988.

Wright, N. T. *After You Believe: Why Christian Character Matters*. New York: HarperOne, 2010.

Wright, N. T. *Surprised by Hope: Rethinking Heaven, the Resurrection, and the Mission of the Church*. New York: HarperOne, 2008.

CPSIA information can be obtained
at www.ICGtesting.com
Printed in the USA
FFHW012315120819
54213113-59941FF